50

WINNING ANSWERS TO INTERVIEW QUESTIONS

EVERYTHING YOU NEED TO KNOW TO PREPARE
YOURSELF FOR THE JOB INTERVIEW

Edited by

Charles F. Albrecht, Jr.

DBM
PUBLISHING

A DIVISION OF DRAKE BEAM MORIN, INC.

New York

CONTENTS

Contents

INTRODUCTION

You are probably reading this book because you are already looking for, or anticipate looking for, a job in the near future. Perhaps you are a recent graduate going after your first real job. You may be at midcareer and seeking a new position out of choice or because your company is downsizing or no longer needs your particular skills. You may even be an early retiree who is not really ready to retire and wants to pursue other career opportunities, perhaps a second career that is very different from your first.

Whatever your situation, you can be sure of one thing: you will be subjected to a number of employment interviews before securing that new position. You will probably be interviewed by several people (perhaps by several at once), each with his or her own personality and set of expectations for successful performance in the position for which you are interviewing.

You can also be sure of something else: your interviewers will ask some tough questions. And in today's highly competitive job market, you must be prepared to answer them in a skillful, credible manner.

But what *is* a "skillful, credible manner"? To address that question, we asked a number of the very people who

1

will be sitting across the desk from you—human resource interviewers and line managers who regularly conduct interviews—how *they* would define the phrase. In their replies, two key phrases kept coming up: the candidate "answers questions honestly" and "knows how to put his (or her) best foot forward."

The skillful employment interviewer asks tough questions because he or she wants to go below the surface to find out what the applicant has really done and how he or she has really behaved in other situations. The interviewer knows that past performance is usually the best predictor of future performance and that, by asking tough questions, he or she will get a better idea of how well the applicant will do in the job and the company. The interviewer's own reputation and/or department is on the line, so he or she is particularly interested in resolving three basic issues:

1. **Can do?** Does the candidate have the necessary skills and experience to handle the responsibilities of the job successfully?
2. **Will do?** Does the candidate possess the motivation to do the job, even if it can be difficult at times and present numerous obstacles?
3. **A good fit?** How well does the candidate's work style fit into the culture of the department or area and into the organization as a whole?

We at Drake Beam Morin know these interviewers' criteria intimately because we're very familiar with the applicant's side of the interview. As the world's largest outplacement firm, we have prepared millions of people to face the tough questions as they interview for employment. The research for this book included an extensive survey of our candidates to identify the most common tough questions they were being asked.

"Why should I have to even think about these answers to the tough questions?" you may ask. "This seems so artificial. Shouldn't my record speak for itself?" Unfortunately, in today's highly competitive job market, a successful track record is rarely enough. You will be competing against many other candidates who have equally impressive track records. And records don't really speak for themselves: **you** have to speak for yourself. It's not always the best-qualified applicants who get the job. It's just as often the applicants who best present their skills and who demonstrate their ability to think on their feet. This may not seem fair, but job candidates who give well-considered yet candid answers to the tough questions are often given higher marks than those who stumble over their answers, contradict themselves, or give pat, overrehearsed replies.

You may be tempted to go right to the center of this book, which contains 50 tough interview questions and suggested approaches for answering them. You may have an interview tomorrow and need some immediate guidance. But if you do, be sure you also read Chapter 1: Preparation and Chapter 3: Following Up. Giving good answers to the tough questions is an important part of interviewing, but it's only one part. You need to prepare in other ways for the interview, and you also need to follow up professionally and thoroughly.

Whatever stage you're at in your career, and whatever type of position you are seeking, you can profit from reading this book and learning from the experiences of thousands of job candidates and interviewers to secure the job of your dreams.

Chapter 1

PREPARING FOR THE INTERVIEW

For most of us, the interview is a stress-producing situation. We're being judged against the standards of the company and the qualifications of the other applicants. It's not something we do very often, and we're conducting this challenging conversation with people we do not even know. This is why, even if your credentials seem to make you a perfect match for the position and you have tremendous poise, it's a good idea to prepare thoroughly for the interview. In getting ready for it, there are two extremes to avoid: doing too little preparation and doing too much.

UNDERPREPARATION

For many years, the unprepared applicant was, by far, the most common. Applicants would show up at interviews without even looking at the company's annual report or knowing the first thing about its products or services. Or they wouldn't know the name of the person who was about to conduct the interview. They would arrive late because they hadn't listened to the directions carefully enough or allowed for rush-hour traffic. They might wear inappropriately casual clothing to a conservative organization, colors that didn't match, or noticeably scuffed shoes. And their answer to a difficult question was likely to be: "Gee, that's a tough one. I never thought about it much. I'm not sure what to tell you."

Every interviewer has more than one story about such applicants. Fortunately, the stories are becoming fewer as applicants become more experienced and sophisticated. But most candidates still need to remind themselves of key preparation techniques.

OVERPREPARATION

The other extreme—the overrehearsed, slick, or glib applicant—is becoming increasingly common. These applicants have the right answer for every question. Their responses are just the right length; they've done research on the company; their diction is superb; and every time the interviewer mentions a particular job responsibility, they cite a prior accomplishment that demonstrates skill in that area. In fact, they answer all the tough questions almost exactly as we recommend in this book.

But an interviewer's impression of such candidates is often that, although technically perfect, their answers are almost too good. Such individuals come across, at least initially, more like robots than people. "She lacked warmth. She wasn't natural," an interviewer may observe. Or, "There was no passion, no spontaneity. He had all the answers, but I got no feel for the real person inside."

In preparing your answers to the tough questions, be sure to avoid this mistake. Don't spend so much time memorizing the lines that you forget to let the interviewer see the real you.

The suggested answers and approaches presented in this book are only guidelines. The actual words you use and the way you say them must mesh with your true personality and the way you naturally handle yourself in most situations. You don't want the interviewer hiring someone who's not really you.

"What a contradiction!" you may be saying. "You emphasize all this practice and preparation, and at the same time tell me to be candid and spontaneous—to think on my feet. How can I do all this without tying myself in knots?"

Ironically, thorough preparation frees you up to be more spontaneous, to show more of the real you. Because the interview itself is, in many ways, an artificial situation, many people's personalities undergo a radical change when they enter the interview room. Normally assertive, detail-oriented people start forgetting things and apologizing for it. Verbally facile people find that the right words don't come easily. Executives who've given difficult presentations to hostile audiences without breaking into a sweat find their palms drenched when asked difficult interview questions for a job they really want.

The prepared candidate avoids these problems. If you have a good idea of your responses to most of the tough questions and have given them some thought and practice, you are more likely to relax and concentrate on being your-self. *The content of your answers will be convincing and appropriate, but you will also be able to answer in a more natural way.*

This is probably the most important part of interview-ing. Most candidates have the credentials and experience ("can do") and motivation ("will do") or they wouldn't have been invited for the interview. What interviewers increas-ingly look for as the deciding factor is the "good-fit" variable: the work style and personality of the applicant and their match with the culture of the work unit and the organization. It's extremely difficult for the interviewer to gauge this fit if your personality never comes across because you're concen-trating on giving the perfect answer to every question.

Do interviewers notice the difference between an over-rehearsed, unnatural approach versus one that shows thoughtful preparation, warmth, and naturalness? You bet they do. Here are a few comments on the subject from interviewers themselves:

"Honesty is what I look for. It's difficult to distin-guish at times. I look for thoughtfulness, sponta-neity, and flow. Body language usually exhibits discomfort or confidence."

"I look for a composed professional and natural response. Good eye contact and plenty of smiles. Also, a person who can feel secure enough to say that a question is tough and requests a moment to think about it. Instantaneous responses are

usually a dead giveaway that the applicant has ready-made answers for any question."

"If candidates seem too slick, I try to trip them up, probe the questions deeper, look for several examples of the skill or behavior they claim to possess."

"How do I know a canned answer? When I've heard it too many times before. I always go two or three probes deeper when I hear one of these answers. You usually can find out if a person's been exaggerating or bluffing."

"I try to ask candidates the same question three different ways. If they are comfortable and really mean what they say, they will be consistent."

The last thing you want to do is memorize every answer to every possible tough question, then turn yourself on like a telephone answering machine with several dozen different tapes. Rather than a script, you need a general approach to answering the questions. When you are confident of your general approach, you are much more likely to give honest answers that highlight your most significant accomplishments. You are also much more likely to be natural, spontaneous, and relaxed than if you were totally unprepared or if you were straining to remember your next "prerecorded" answer.

THE VALUE OF PRACTICING AHEAD OF TIME

There's an old joke about a street musician who's approached by a tourist and asked, "How do you get to Carnegie Hall?" The answer: "Practice, practice, practice!" Most of us have had precious little practice at interviewing. A generation ago, when people often stayed with one company their entire career, one interview was the limit of many people's entire experience. It's more the norm today for someone to have had several employers over the course of a career, but that still means that a job interview is not exactly an everyday, reflexive occurrence.

Practicing Your Delivery

It can be extremely helpful to practice before an interview. Some people practice using a videotape, with a friend or spouse playing the role of interviewer. Others practice alone, facing a mirror. The important thing is to give yourself a "dry run," both verbally and visually, before the actual event. This enables you to try out your answers and modify them if you or the person giving feedback is not satisfied. It also gives you valuable feedback on *how* you're delivering your answers. Are you responding too quickly and automatically? Are you relaxed and thoughtful? Do you have annoying verbal or nonverbal mannerisms?

Finally, how do you look and feel? Have you finalized your clothing and accessory choices—from suit, shirt/blouse, shoes, and coat, to tie, jewelry, briefcase, and/or handbag? Is everything wrinkle-free and ready to go? Does it fit as well sitting down as standing up? And, most important, do you feel comfortable and confident wearing it? A practice interview in the clothes you plan to wear will ensure that no last-minute details have to be ironed out—either literally or figuratively—in the psychologically critical hour before you set off for the interview.

Practicing the Reversal Technique

Another technique you can practice that produces a win-win situation for both interviewer and interviewee is called the *reversal*. The goal of an interview should be not a one-way monologue by the interviewer or an interrogation in which you simply answer questions nonstop, but rather a relaxed, two-way conversation in which you both get to speak. The reversal accomplishes this. By ending your answer to a question with a question of your own, you indicate that you have been listening and want to know more about the organization. You get some of the information you need, avoid embarrassing silences, and give yourself a little extra breathing time before the interviewer asks the next question and you go onstage again. Here's an example:

INTERVIEWER: What is your experience in leading teams?

CANDIDATE: We began the transition to teams several years ago on a selective basis. My area was not one of the first selected, so I had a chance to observe other areas' successes and problems. My own area began to work officially as a team about six months ago. We've been able to avoid getting so absorbed in the process that we forget to look for results. But one of our problems has been holding individuals accountable for team processes. Have you encountered that problem here?

Interviewer: I'm glad you brought that up. That's been one of our biggest problems as well. How can you do a fair performance evaluation on a person when the team has failed to achieve objectives for which that person is being held responsible?

Making the Practice Trip

Another aspect of practice that is sometimes overlooked is a practice trip to the site of the interview. Of course, if the interview is in another city, this may be impractical. But if it is reasonably near your home and you have a strong interest in the position, it will probably be worth your while to make a practice run. This can help you gauge the time necessary to arrive at the interview and familiarize yourself with the facility and any time-consuming security procedures you may encounter there. You may also be able to pick up an annual report or other materials about the company (such as marketing materials or product brochures) or perhaps even obtain a copy of the application form so that you can complete it at home prior to the interview.

There is nothing worse than getting lost on the way to an interview or arriving late because you didn't know which parking lot to park in or went to the wrong building and had to go through security twice. Most of us lose our composure to some degree in such situations, and you don't want to arrive at the interview feeling frazzled. The practice trip can all but eliminate the likelihood of such an occurrence.

QUESTIONS *YOU* CAN ASK DURING THE INTERVIEW

The reversal technique is best used when you have thought about the questions to which you really would like answers. It's not a game; it's an information exchange. Ideally, you are getting many of your questions answered during the interview. When the interviewer concludes by asking, "Do you have any questions I haven't answered?" you will only have one or two left. It's best not to end the session by interrogating the interviewer with an endless list of questions you could have raised during the course of the interview.

What are these questions? There is no set list; it depends on the nature of the position and the types of questions whose answers are most important to you. Here are some of the questions applicants most frequently ask and find useful:

1. Why is this position open?
2. How often has it been filled in the past five or ten years?
3. What have been the primary reasons for people leaving?
4. What can the person who fills the job do differently from the person who is leaving?
5. What are the most important long-term objectives for the person filling the job?
6. What are the most pressing needs for the job in the first few months?

7. How much freedom is there in determining work objectives, deadlines, and methods of measurement?

8. What are the measures of success and how would I be evaluated?

9. What are the most difficult problems facing the person in this position? How have they been handled in the past, and what approach might work best in the future?

10. What kind of support does this position receive in terms of finances, equipment, staff?

11. What would be a typical career path for someone who is successful in this position? Where could one go and what would be a realistic time frame?

12. How would you characterize the culture of the organization? Could you give me a few examples of how I would see that culture manifested?

13. What has been the organization's biggest success in the last five years? Its biggest misstep?

14. What significant changes do you foresee in the near future?

15. What are the most critical factors for success in this position? In this organization?

16. How would you describe your own management style? (if the interviewer would be the candidate's manager)

17. What are the most important traits you look for in a subordinate? (again, if the interviewer would be the candidate's manager)

18. How do you like people to communicate with you? Orally or in writing, formally or informally?

19. Can you describe the political climate in the organization?

20. How are decisions made and problems solved?

21. What is the normal work pace compared to other companies in this industry?

22. To what degree is creativity encouraged or discouraged?

23. With which departments would I be working most closely? How would you describe the current relationships with those departments?

24. How is information shared within the organization?

Don't rely on this list of questions alone. There are probably a number of additional questions the answers to which are especially important to you or are unique to the particular position for which you're applying. You'll want to jot those down or have them clearly in mind when you enter.

It's particularly important that you understand where you stand and what the next steps in the selection process will be. These end-of-interview questions are critical. However, many people overlook them because of the stress of the interview or because they don't know how to phrase them gracefully. "Did I get the job?" or "Where do I stand?" are pretty blunt questions, and the interviewer probably can't answer either of them at the time of the interview.

Here are some well-phrased end-of-interview questions you *can* ask:

1. What are the next steps?
2. What is the timing?
3. How many people are you planning to interview?
4. Where am I in the interview sequence?
5. How will you notify candidates who have been selected for the next step in the process?

DOING YOUR HOMEWORK

You will want to know as much as possible about the company, the job, and the manager before you enter the interview. To do that, thorough research is necessary. However, you want to be careful and tactful in revealing what you know about the company and how you got the information.

When asked, "What do you know about our company?" you will not leave a very good impression by answering, "Well, I know you manufacture medical devices, but that's about it." But the impression may be even worse if you say, "Fortunately, I know Sally Rodriguez in your research area. So I know that the Easy-Walk prosthetic device is being cancelled and that the optimistic projections in your annual report will have to be modified."

You want to reveal enough information so that the interviewer realizes you've made a good-faith effort to learn about the company. But you don't want to come across as arrogant or someone who divulges confidences (Sally's information on the Easy-Walk device may just be hearsay or a plan that has not received final approval). If you give the impression that you really do already "know it all," you'll leave the interviewer with little to tell you. It's better to give some broad-brush statements of what you know and follow them up with questions about specifics. Says one human resource interviewer, "We would give bad marks to anyone who didn't know what we were all about. At the very least, you should make a trip to the library and read the company's annual report."

Here is some of the background information you will want to obtain ahead of time:

1. Industry information: historic and recent trends, noteworthy companies, and top competitors

2. Company information: history, growth rate, size; profitability; products and services; financial history and current status; top management players (backgrounds, tenure/average age, philosophy; company culture; changes in structure and actual or planned downsizings; changes in products, service lines, and/or general strategy

3. Departmental information: work pace and style in the department; boss's personality and management style; recent or contemplated personnel changes; new technologies being introduced

There are two basic ways to get this background information: (1) networking; and (2) published research.

Research Via Networking

Networking is the art of contacting people you already know to obtain information about organizations and people you don't know. You may not know anyone who works at the company or who is familiar with the area in which you would be working. However, you can question colleagues, extended family and/or their friends, people you know from your community, and members of trade or religious organizations to see if they know anyone who works at the company and/or knows about the position in question. Anyone who has had some contact with that company is a possible source of information, even if they have been a customer or a vendor. Networking is usually the best way to get subjective information—views and opinions about the field and the company from a personal perspective.

Research Via Published Sources

Published materials are usually the best source of hard, objective data. The offices of outplacement firms like Drake Beam Morin usually have research libraries to give their candidates access to annual reports, business and trade association directories, and business and general journals and newspapers. In addition, they may subscribe to a number of databases that provide up-to-date information on target companies. A research librarian is often available to do searches for articles on a particular company. Abstracts of these or their full texts can be gathered quickly for candidates, particularly when they have an interview the next day.

If you do not have the services of an outplacement firm, you can still do research, but you will have to make proactive use of the resources in your community. Visit your library, explain your situation to the librarian, and ask him or her to teach you about the published and computerized research sources available and their use. Read local and national business periodicals and trade journals, looking for mention of the company at which you will be interviewing and making notes on company direction, key executives, problems they are grappling with, financial trends, and the company's plans for expanding, contracting or modifying products and services.

Research Via the Practice Visit

Another way to research a company is to be carefully observant during your practice visit. While you are there, pick up the annual report and any company newsletters (these are usually on a table in the human resources department). Are you subjected to a thorough security check? Are you asked to sign in or are you just pointed down the hall? Are people dressed formally or informally? Is the atmosphere quiet or charged with activity? Look in the display cases and at the bulletin boards; the information there can give you a quick read on what the company considers important.

Research Via Company Ads and Customer Feedback

You can also study a company's advertising. Read print ads to see how the company is positioning itself and its products or services, and be prepared to ask how this approach is working. If the company manufactures or distributes products, visit a retail outlet to see how these are featured and displayed. You can also talk to people who've used the company's product or services, paying particular attention to benefits and competitive advantages.

MANAGING PRE-INTERVIEW STRESS

Most people find the interview situation at least moderately stressful. You have about an hour to prove to a total stranger that you are competent, motivated, and a good fit with the job and the company. You may feel that your entire professional career hangs in the balance. Meanwhile, you are expected to be calm, smiley, and friendly during this interchange, to be your best self, and to be prepared to answer any question the interviewer asks.

You probably won't experience as much stress as one candidate who was so nervous that he found himself trembling even during his *practice* interviews with his outplacement counselor. But you will probably experience some stress, and we want to suggest some techniques specifically geared to reducing the anxiety that often accompanies interviews.

Taking Good Care of Yourself the Day Before

It's important to eat right, sleep well, and do something pleasurable the day leading up to the interview. Many people tend to do just the opposite; they approach an interview in the same way they crammed for an exam in college. They eat large amounts of nonnutritious junk food and stay up too late poring over their research. It's questionable whether such behavior really improves performance on a written exam. It certainly does not enhance performance at an interview, where you must not only know your facts but also be personally engaging.

The day before an important interview, eat three nutritious meals. Avoid drinking the night before in an effort to relax. Engage in an enjoyable, relaxing activity, preferably one that allows physical release of tension, such as a visit to your health club or a run of a couple of miles. (No marathons; you'll need some energy to spare!) That way, you'll be pleasantly tired and get a good night's sleep. Give your research a once-over, but don't try to cram it into your head or memorize it till all hours of the morning.

Visualizing the Interview in Advance

One particularly useful ploy is mental rehearsal. In this technique, you visualize the interview proceeding exactly the way you wish it to go — just as if it were actually happening. In effect, you create your own mental movie of the event in advance. This technique is often used by actors and athletes before crucial performances or contests. Swimmers envision themselves touching the edge of the pool before everyone else. Divers envision the perfect dive and see themselves making a splashless entry into the water. A pianist imagines herself gliding effortlessly through a fiendishly difficult passage and finishing to tumultuous applause. Does this sound like voodoo? Just ask the people who use the technique successfully!

Unfortunately, what most of us tend to do before a stress-producing event like an interview is just the opposite of a positive mental rehearsal; we engage in negative visualization. We see ourselves making some foolish mistake, getting caught by a trick question, and somehow blowing all our chances for the job.

It's a lot more effective to imagine the whole scenario in terms of success. Start by seeing yourself leaving the house well-dressed and confident, your briefcase not stuffed but containing key materials. See yourself finding the building easily and arriving a few minutes ahead of schedule. See yourself greeting the interviewer in a confident manner, asking and answering questions (even the tough ones) in a calm, relaxed fashion. See yourself smiling, shaking hands with interviewer, and leaving with the knowledge that you've handled yourself well. And since you've carried the visualization this far, why not take it to the max and see yourself starting your new job!

This type of visualization is easier if you have something to base it on. So it's a good idea to mentally review all the successes and accomplishments you'll be talking about in the interview. This is called *success bombardment*. Don't just mechanically check off or list all your successes. Relive them. Visualize them. Savor them. Remember the high you felt when you accomplished them. Get out that award-winning portfolio or the congratulatory letter from the chairman. When the interviewer asks, "What was your biggest success?" you'll be ready with an answer that's not only factual but also reflects the commitment and enthusiasm that so many interviewers look for (and so many stressed-out interviewees fail to convey).

Using Relaxation Techniques

In addition to visualizations that specifically target the interview situation, there are several good general relaxation exercises. The first one, *progressive relaxation*, is primarily physical. Edmund Jacobson, a researcher at the University of Chicago in the 1930s, discovered that when a muscle was deliberately tensed and then released, the resulting relaxation was greater than before the muscle was tensed. Furthermore, people could actually train themselves to progressively relax.

In progressive relaxation, you start by tensing the muscles in your feet, consciously holding the tension for a few seconds, and then letting go, allowing your feet to relax completely. You will find that your feet feel more relaxed than the rest of your body. Then follow the same procedure for your calves, and you will find that feet and calves are more relaxed than the rest of the body. By the time you have progressed all the way up to your head, you will be completely relaxed.

Other visualizations are primarily mental. One technique is the beach visualization, in which you close your eyes and imagine yourself at the beach. The visualization makes use of all the senses: you "smell" the salt air, "hear" the crashing of the waves and the crying of the gulls, "taste" the saltwater, "touch" the dry, warm sand, and "see" fluffy white clouds and green dune grass. Similar visualizations can be done using other calming settings, like a mountain meadow or a forest clearing.

"But where am I supposed to perform these techniques?" you might ask. "I can't just nod out in the waiting room." Many candidates find that the perfect time to do these exercises is at home, just before leaving for the interview, on public transportation, or in the parking lot before entering the site of the interview.

DRESSING FOR THE OCCASION

There's been a lot of emphasis on business dress and image in the past decade, and for good reason. While the idea of dressing appropriately for an interview is universally accepted, exactly what that means can vary widely from company to company, region to region. Styles are always changing, and what's considered appropiate for a 25-year-old copywriter may not be considered appropriate for a 50-year-old accountant. It's also true that even if you're the world's greatest financial analyst or programmer, an interviewer may have trouble believing it if your appearance is unprofessional. Because the interview is a brief meeting (and you may not be invited back), you literally only have one chance to make a first impression. Many of the interviewers surveyed for this book told us that they can tell whether a candidate is worth interviewing during the first

30 seconds. That judgment is usually made on the basis of appearance and how the candidate handles him or herself in those 30 seconds.

Why all the fuss about appearance? Isn't the most important criterion your ability to do the job? Yes, say interviewers, but if your appearance is unkempt or inappropriate, it may speak so loudly that the interviewer's ability to listen to your abilities and credentials suffers. "Your goal should be to stand out, not stick out," says one interviewer. "Once I've noticed that you have a polished, professional appearance, I can move on to the more important factors— skills, motivation, fit. But if your shoes are scuffed or you're wearing a purple shirt, I can be distracted by that throughout the interview and the focus won't be where it should."

What are some of the pet peeves of corporate interviewers?

- "Ponytails, particularly on men."
- "Sagging ankle socks."
- "Scuffed, down-at-the-heel shoes. It's the one thing men in particular sometimes neglect, and I see it as lack of attention to detail."
- "Polyester ties and shirts on candidates for professional positions."
- "Heaps of jewelry that bangs, clangs, and glitters."
- "Women who dress provocatively; it's distracting for interviewers of both sexes."
- "Untrimmed beards and moustaches."
- "Too much perfume or cologne."

General Guidelines

To get an idea of the accepted dress at the organization, you can look at the annual report to see how people at various levels dress. You can also visit the workplace. Observe how people appear and what they are wearing when they arrive at work (they may not look as good at the end of the day) and go to your interview looking just a little bit better. After all, you're trying to make your best impression. Notes one interviewer, "If a person is inappropriately dressed for the interview, I know it's only going to get worse once he or she is on the job." Above all, say most interviewers, you should be comfortable with your own package. When in doubt, err on the conservative side; it's better to appear too staid than to give the impression that you're too loose and not really serious.

What does this conservative dress usually look like? For the majority of office positions, you can't go wrong if you follow these guidelines:

- A dark (grey, blue, brown), conservatively cut business suit for both men and women. For men, a white or blue shirt; stripes are a little riskier and some men don't match suits, ties and striped shirts well. The shirt should be all or mostly cotton. For women, a shirt or blouse of any color that goes well with the suit. The fabric should complement the suit. Cotton, silk or rayon are generally acceptable for executive or professional positions; polyester is okay for administrative jobs.

- Accessories should be unobtrusive and complement the rest of the outfit. No heavy jewelry for either sex. Watches should be of good quality and present a business image. No gold chains for men. No dangly earrings (studs are more appropriate) or jangly bracelets for women. Belts should match shoes and should not have an oversize, distracting buckle. Paisley ties are generally too loud, but men are no longer restricted to solids, dots, or stripes.
- For men, dark socks and well-shined shoes. Lace-ups are more conservative than loafers, and many interviewers feel that penny loafers in particular are too informal. Women have more leeway, but shoes should be businesslike, should complement the rest of the outfit, and should not have open toes.

Note that these are general recommendations only. Business styles are changing more rapidly than in previous generations, and your outfit should be tailored to the environment in which you will be interviewing and (hopefully) working. It should also be appropriate to the position for which you're applying and to your age and stage in your career. Regional differences may also come into play.

Company Culture Determinants

The company culture is particularly important in determining what to wear. In some companies, you may be instantly branded a maverick if you show up in anything other than a navy suit, white shirt, striped tie, and wing-tips. In others, this may type you as hopelessly unimaginative and uncreative. Interviewers complain frequently about new graduates who are used to wearing jeans on campus and who think a sports jacket with contrasting slacks constitutes formal business dress.

But it's not just young people who fail to comply with a company's dress customs at interviews. Older applicants often make similar mistakes, particularly if they've been with one company for many years and are used to dressing for that company or a particular department within it. For instance, one executive left a blue-chip Fortune 500 company and was interviewing at a much smaller company that had few of the trappings of his former employer. He showed up in an expensive suit, Hermes tie, and Gucci loafers. He was even still wearing his old company tie pin. Most of the people he was interviewing with were wearing slacks, sweaters, and running shoes. Their impression? Here was a person whose head, heart, and soul were still at his old company. He was also probably too status-conscious for this informal, egalitarian company where everyone was expected to roll up his or her sleeves and do whatever needed to be done.

Dress-Down-Day Exceptions

Another pitfall is the ever-more-popular dress-down day. This can fall on a particular day of the week—usually Friday—or last an entire season (usually summer). (It can also seem totally random.) It's increasingly common for applicants to arrive at the interview in their best suit only to find everyone else in jeans. One candidate arrived at an interview without being told that Friday was dress-down day. The person who greeted him in the lobby looked like a lumberjack but was actually the vice president to whom he would be reporting. When the applicant started apologizing for being over-dressed, the vice president explained that *he* felt *under-dressed* and hoped the applicant would understand.

Another applicant encountered a similar situation, ex-cept that she had been scheduled to give a presentation to a group of employees as part of her interview process. The participants were all dressed casually and invited the appli-cant to have a slice of pizza from a box on the table. After sharing this informal meal with the participants, she under-standably modified the formal approach of her presentation. Her feedback? The presentation had been too informal con-sidering the highly sophisticated, formal environments in which she would be expected to do presentations as a member of the company.

Particularly if you know the organization has a reputa-tion for informality, it's a good idea to ask the person you'll be interviewing with if there are any dress-down days. If one of them is the day you're to be interviewed, ask if it's appro-priate for applicants to dress down also. If it is, get a feel for what most people wear on dress down day and dress at least a notch above that. For instance, if most people will be wearing jeans, wear a skirt with a nice sweater or a sport coat and slacks.

Dressing for a Particular Position

The position for which you're applying is another important determinant of how you will dress. Says one interviewer at a computer company, "Writers should look as if they'd just come out of a bar. Account executives should wear classics with a twist; colorful blazers, soft wool pants." Says another at a Big Six accounting firm, "It never ceases to amaze me that a kid right out of college shows up in a $500 suit and $75 tie, wearing a $1,000 watch. Not only is it unnecessary, it's inappropriate. Most of our partners don't dress like that. This kid's first job is probably going to be taking inventory of boxes of fabric in a factory. I usually ask someone dressed like that if he is aware of what he'll be doing in his first few years with the firm."

You should try to dress like someone occupying the position you wish to fill. If you are going to be a beginning accountant, don't dress better than the client's CEO or the partner in charge of the audit. On the other hand, if you are applying for the position of account executive at an advertising agency, you may want to present an image that matches your clients'. Back-office jobs generally demand less formal or dynamic dress than positions with frequent client contact.

Taking Account of Age and Regional Factors

Your age can be a factor in dressing appropriately. Because interviewers sometimes stereotype younger people as impulsive, a younger applicant may want to dress very conservatively to dispel this image. For older applicants a splash of color and style can do wonders to convey a more youthful, energetic image. "I hate to say it," says one interviewer, "but when you've got a person with grey socks, a grey suit, and grey hair, well, they sometimes leave a grey impression." If you're an older applicant, this may be the perfect time to spruce up that tired old wardrobe with some brightly colored accessories: suspenders, handkerchiefs, brighter ties with slightly bolder patterns and, for women, brightly colored blouses.

Regional differences need to be honored, too. If you're a Texan interviewing with a firm in New York, you probably want to leave your cowboy boots at home. And if you're a New Yorker interviewing in Miami in the summer, they just might think you're a stuffed shirt if the one you're wearing has long sleeves.

If you've followed the suggestions in this section of the book, you've practiced your interviewing skills and your trip to the interviewing site. You know which questions you're going to ask. You are prepared with techniques to combat stress. You even know what you're going to wear. The only thing left you need to know before the interview is some suggested approaches to answering the tough questions. And that is exactly what you'll learn in the next section.

Chapter 2

50 TOUGH INTERVIEW QUESTIONS

The tough questions and great answers that follow draw on Drake Beam Morin's more than 25 years of coaching and training people on both sides of the interviewing desk. Remember, for the most part we will be giving you approaches, not scripted answers. Interviewers, you will remember, usually see through candidates who simply mouth prepared scripts. So you'll need to tailor the specific wording of your answers to fit your background, the situation, and the position for which you're interviewing.

The approaches we recommend have been used successfully by many candidates and have also been reviewed for their appropriateness in a survey of interviewers. By using them flexibly, you will be seen as a candidate who has prepared well but can answer in a spontaneous, nonscripted manner. You will have a distinct advantage over the person who is unprepared or who has merely memorized a set of canned answers.

1

"TELL ME ABOUT YOURSELF."

This classic question can be particularly tough to answer if you have not prepared for it. To add to the pressure, it's often the first question asked, before you've had a chance to establish rapport with the interviewer. Why do interviewers often choose to begin with such a seemingly general question? What's their agenda in asking it? How much do they really want to know?

Most interviewers want to know if you are able to give a brief, sequential summary of your life and career that relates to the job for which you're interviewing. They want to see if you ramble or include large amounts of irrelevant information. They want to get a feel for your conversational style, your confidence level, your ability to organize and present information. And they want to get an idea of the person you are behind the suit.

There are two major errors you can make here. One is to answer in a sentence or two, either because you are unprepared or because you figure that the interviewer can learn more about you by asking other questions besides "Tell me about yourself."

The other error is to "blither," as one interviewer puts it. "I had one applicant whom I had to stop after seven minutes; he was only up to high school," she chuckles. "He created the impression of someone who lacks focus, and he certainly wasn't reading my nonverbal signals that he was going on far too long about irrelevant information. He even told me about his difficulty in training his dog."

You should prepare a two-minute presentation (about 250 words) that includes a brief introduction (perhaps where you were born and raised, your education, and your personality strengths), your work history, and recent career experience. The most time should be spent on the accomplishments in the latter two areas. (One candidate made his presentation easier to follow by dividing his career into segments: formative, middle, and recent.) Remember that your accomplishments reflect your strengths; your answer to this initial question is your opportunity to point the interview in the direction that you want it to go, by focusing on your strengths, as this is what is most pertinent to the needs of any prospective employer.

You don't want to sound as if you've memorized your presentation, and are just repeating it word for word, so remember to maintain a conversational tone. Keep an eye on the interviewer for any nonverbal clues that the answer is going on too long or that more information is desired.

2

"WHAT DO YOU KNOW ABOUT OUR ORGANIZATION?"

If you have performed your research thoroughly, using both networking and published sources, you should be able to discuss the company's products, services, revenues, reputation, culture, mission and goals, history, geographical distribution of people and facilities. However, you shouldn't act as if you know everything about the organization: you can't and don't. While your answer should show that you have taken the time to do some research, you don't want to overwhelm the interviewer with your encyclopedic knowledge of the organization. You may be wrong on some points and you may also appear arrogant.

Make it clear that while you have done your homework on the organization, you want to learn more from those who know most about it, the current employees, particularly the person across the desk from you. Keep your answer positive. Don't say, "Everyone tells me that you're in a precarious position, losing market share rapidly, and no one seems to know what to do about it." Even if this is true, your interviewer will probably not appreciate such a blunt and negative comment.

"I really don't expect an applicant to have memorized a lot of facts and figures about the company," says one interviewer. "The important thing is that he or she has taken the effort to do some research on us and wants to learn more."

3

"WHY DO YOU WANT TO WORK FOR US?"

Here the interviewer is probing for your motivation for joining the company. Are you just seeking a bigger paycheck and more benefits? Is the situation so terrible at your present company that anything would be an improvement? Perceptive interviewers don't just take your answer at face value; they have experience in reading between the lines.

Your answer should therefore reflect your desire to contribute to the company and grow as a professional. You should have done enough research on the company to point out the areas in which its needs and your skills are a good match. Point out unique approaches, products, or services the company offers and cite how your experience prepares you to contribute to the company's mission. If the company has a mission statement, you can refer to this as it relates to your skills, business philosophy, and career goals.

If your research has shown that the company is strong on research and development, talk about how you've always worked well in that area and give examples. If you know that the company likes to be a leader in the marketplace, say that this is attractive to you and give examples of instances when you helped introduce a new product or service.

There are a number of weak answers to this question, and interviewers indicate that they hear them more than they would like. One is, "I really like working with people."

Every company has people, so you're not really addressing why this particular company is a good match for your skills and interests. Another weak approach is to emphasize what a wonderful place the company would be to work for because of its good salaries, liberal benefits, and vacation time, and people-oriented culture. This merely emphasizes what you hope to *get* from the company, not what you are prepared to contribute. It can be mentioned briefly, but the bulk of your answer should address contributions you hope to make.

If you can't think of a good answer to this question, you need to do more research on the company and/or analysis of what you have to offer before you go on the interview. If you still can't come up with a good answer, perhaps this organization really isn't for you.

4

"WHY ARE YOU LEAVING (DID YOU LEAVE) YOUR PRESENT (LAST) POSITION?"

Most interviewers do not want to hear about how awful your boss was, the unfairness of the downsizing, or the bitter battle between two bosses that resulted in one of their protégés moving ahead and you being left without a future. "What I look for is not so much the reason for leaving as I do how the applicant describes it," notes one interviewer. "Is he still dealing with bitter or sad feelings, or has he been able to focus his energy on the future and the next position? Does he place total blame on others for his situation or does he accept at least some responsibility for it?"

It's best to be brief and to the point. "The more an individual talks about this, the more I assume that she is fixated on it, or that she is talking around an issue that she would rather hide," notes another interviewer. You can make this question easier to answer by working out a departure statement with your employer that you both agree to stick to.

If you were laid off as part of a downsizing or staff reduction, say so. "My position was eliminated as part of a downsizing," is a brief answer that will satisfy most interviewers; if they ask another question, respond to that one briefly as well.

If your move is a voluntary one, give your reasons, not

in terms of your dissatisfaction at your current job, but rather in terms of the contributions you would like to make at the new company.

If you were actually terminated, be as positive and honest as you can. Many terminations, particularly at executive levels, are based on fit, not performance, so you may want to use that term in your answer. "Fit" is always a better term than "personality conflict"; the interviewer may conclude that you will find personalities to conflict with at her organization as well. If you have established the impression of a good fit with this organization, you are in a better position to discuss fit as a factor in leaving your old organization, particularly if the organizations have different cultures.

5

"WHAT CAN YOU DO FOR US THAT SOMEONE ELSE CAN'T?"

(Variations on this question are, "What do you bring to the table that's unique?" or "Why should we hire you?")

Your answer should be based on your knowledge of the job, the company, and the "hot buttons" or concerns that you know exist. You also should know exactly what you have to offer that meets the organization's most immediate needs. This is called the *unique selling proposition*, or USP.

This is no time to be modest. Talk about your record of getting things done in areas which relate directly to the most pressing needs in the department and organization. Give specific examples from your resume or record of accomplishments. If organizational skills have been mentioned as a key hiring criterion, mention several instances in which your abilities helped your employer reach important objectives. If computer literacy has been mentioned several times and you know that you are more computer literate than most people in your field, tell about the software programs you are familiar with and give examples of how you used them to enhance a project or general operations.

If you have a special skill that truly sets you apart from others, now is the time to mention it. Here's an example:

"You mentioned that you are aggressively entering the Spanish-speaking market. I speak fluent Spanish, and conducted a telephone marketing survey of Spanish-speaking customers at my last job. So your objectives are perfectly in line with a skill that I enjoy using and hope to develop further."

6

"WHAT DO YOU FIND MOST ATTRACTIVE ABOUT THIS POSITION? WHAT SEEMS LEAST ATTRACTIVE ABOUT IT?"

List at least three or four attractive features of the job, emphasizing that because it is a good match with many of your skills, you will be able to make a maximum contribution. As for unattractive features, mention one or two. They should be minor compared to the positives you have just mentioned, but they should be substantial enough so that the interviewer doesn't feel you are just glossing over the question or are being unrealistic about the job.

In listing any negative, mention how you would act (or have acted in the past) to soften the impact of these negatives or to work around them. For example:

"I know this job involves a lot of travel, and that realistically this can cut into productivity and also limits contact with the rest of the team back at the office. I generally call in at the end of every day to make sure I stay in touch with what's going on. Also, since I got my laptop, I've found a way to put that travel time to better use, even when I'm stuck on the ground in an airport."

7

"WHAT DO YOU LOOK FOR IN A JOB?"

(A variation is "What would be your ideal job?")

The interviewer is looking to see if you have thought about what you enjoy and what you are best at. He or she also wants to know that there is a reasonably good fit between your skills and interests and the job.

Your answer should therefore be made with this job in mind. It's tempting to describe your ideal job by letting your imagination soar to ridiculous heights, but this will probably create something that bears little relation to reality. It's also rather transparent (and also unoriginal) to simply review the job description for the position at hand and then say, "That's exactly what I'm looking for."

A better approach is to give a general breakdown of the types of activities you'd like to engage in. Here's an example:

> *"I'm looking for a job that would use all of my abilities in the training area—delivery, needs analysis, and design. This job appears to offer the opportunity to do all three. What percentages of each do you envision?"*

You also will want to address the type of culture you work best in, giving examples from past experience, and relate this to your research of the organization and the department. Keep your answer oriented to the realistic opportunities at the organization, as well as to your desire to contribute and make a difference.

8

"WHAT DO YOU EXPECT OUT OF THIS POSITION AND YOUR ASSOCIATION WITH OUR COMPANY?"

Although the question as stated really asks, "What's in it for you, Mr. or Ms. Candidate?" you should answer primarily in terms of what you have to offer. Emphasize your desire to contribute and be part of the team, to increase your professional expertise, and to use your skills and knowledge to help accomplish the company's mission. Citing your research and networking contacts, say that, at this stage in your career, this company seems to offer the best opportunity to do this.

Here's an example of a good answer to this question:

"I would like the opportunity to help the company bring innovative products and services to the market before others have had the chance. From my research, I know that you were one of the first banks in this area to introduce ATM's and bank-at-home services. I would want to help you develop and market other new products and services. I would expect to be associated with a market leader, and I find that much more exciting than being with a market follower."

9

"WHAT IS YOUR MANAGEMENT STYLE, AND HOW WOULD YOU RATE YOURSELF AS A MANAGER?"

Your answer should reflect your knowledge of the company's culture and the management style that works best within it. If your management style is diametrically opposed to the company's, you are in the wrong place. If there are enough commonalities to ensure a basic fit, these should be emphasized.

Most successful managers have a good mix of people- and task-orientation. They help the team focus on the task and get the job done. But they are not so task-focused that they forget the human needs of their subordinates. They adjust to and allow for personality differences and keep people motivated to accomplish the tasks.

If the organization at which you're interviewing has a strong team approach, you must pay particular attention to your answer. In such organizations, there is less emphasis on the traditional tasks of management (directing, planning, organizing, controlling) and more on leadership (enabling the team to work together, set their own targets, devise new work approaches). In the past, managers not only set the goals but told subordinates exactly how to accomplish them. The new leader helps the group set goals and encourages them to arrive at their own solutions.

If you know that the organization is making a transition to or is already in this new "team mode," emphasize your experience with it. If you have little experience but a keen interest and desire to lead in such an environment, emphasize the traits you possess that would make you a good team leader, giving examples of those traits in action.

10

"HOW WOULD YOU DESCRIBE YOUR PERSONALITY?"

This is a tricky one. To describe yourself in glowing terms makes you sounds arrogant; listing too many faults weakens your candidacy. "A cliché answer like 'firm but fair' is basically a nonanswer to me," states one interviewer. "It just means I have to ask the question again in a different way or ask for examples."

Try to answer this question with the job requirements firmly in mind. Mention the aspects of your personality that best fit with the job, show how you think they're relevant to the job, and give examples of these traits in action. It's also good to support your statements with feedback you've received from subordinates, peers, and superiors.

Mention one or two minor aspects of your personality that you are dissatisfied with or that have not served you well. If possible, choose traits that relate less closely to the position at hand (lack of detail-orientation may indeed be a minor flaw if your job involves broad-brush strategic thinking and you will have an administrative assistant to help with details). Mention the steps you have taken to improve your behavior in these areas. This could involve formal developmental programs or a developmental plan based on your performance appraisal. Give examples of how your changed behavior has helped achieve departmental or organizational goals.

11

"TELL ME ABOUT YOUR SKILL AS A LEADER."

To answer this question, it's important to know the company's culture. Hopefully, you have some clues from your research and from statements the interviewer has made so far. But it may be useful to ask what the definition of leadership is at this organization. If it is defined as directing, planning, organizing, and controlling, you will want to focus on those areas. If it is more concerned with collaboratively facilitating team efforts, you should emphasize your accomplishments in that mode. Always give examples, since unsupported statements about your "dynamism" or "charisma" will probably seem self-serving.

Here's how one candidate responded to this question:

"A leader today can't just tell people what to do. She has to galvanize other people to act around her ideas. And you've got to overcome resistance and obstacles too. For instance, I came up with the idea of sending out our training manuals on disk to our local offices. That way, they could be printed out at those local offices, eliminating the need for storage and shipping of bulky binders. But I had to overcome the resistance of some administrative assistants, who thought this would mean more work for them. I convinced

them that having to print out a manual once in a while was better than having to order them and then wait for them to be sent from the corporate warehouse. Once the project was underway, I also took the initiative to hire a programmer to format the disks in a way that all our offices could print them out easily."

12

"WHAT DO YOU LOOK FOR WHEN YOU HIRE PEOPLE?"

Your interviewer wants to know if you are a good judge of character and effectiveness on the job. A manager is only as good as the people he or she selects for the team. Moreover, the interviewer may have to work with these people too.

Professional interviewers (and many managers) know that there are three basic criteria for hiring people, whatever the level and position: can do?, will do?, and good fit? Your answer should include mention of all three of them: Does the individual possess the right background and skills (can do)? Is the individual motivated to perform the job (will do)? And will the individual be able to comfortably and productively work with the rest of the team (good fit)?

Give examples of how you have used each of these criteria when hiring people in the past, and how the people selected became contributing members of the team. If some of the people you selected were able to move higher in the organization, you will want to mention this also.

13

"HAVE YOU EVER HAD TO FIRE PEOPLE? WHAT WERE THE REASONS, AND HOW DID YOU HANDLE THE SITUATION?"

There are two extremes to avoid here: depicting yourself as a manager who has never fired anyone because of lack of experience or fear of confrontation, and depicting yourself as a manager who actually enjoys firing people. ("You'd be amazed at the number of managers who say right up front, 'It gave me the greatest pleasure in the world to fire that bastard,'" notes one interviewer. "I'm not generally impressed.")

The interviewer wants to know that you are capable of confronting people about poor performance or inappropriate conduct and can exercise progressive discipline, terminating individuals if necessary. Admit that the situation wasn't easy or pleasant, but that terminating people is part of the job of managing and that you handled it well.

You will do best to pick a case you did indeed handle well (many managers have other cases, especially early in their careers, which make interesting listening but are better left unmentioned). Stress how you followed formal procedure and communicated with the individual throughout the process, pointing out the behaviors that needed changing and giving the person the opportunity to change them. If your actions also minimized negative reactions from the remaining staff or avoided threatened legal action, state how that was achieved.

"WHAT DO YOU THINK IS THE MOST DIFFICULT THING ABOUT BEING A MANAGER (ENGINEER, ACCOUNT EXECUTIVE, ETC.)?"

The interviewer wants to know if you have thought about the difficulties inherent in your job, how you've handled them in the past, and what steps, if any, you're taking to deal with these difficulties better. A good answer emphasizes major difficulties you've actually experienced. That way you can also give an example of how you successfully handled a particular difficulty.

If you have taken specific steps to deal with these difficulties (a course in conflict management, for example), now is a good time to mention this. Never mention a difficulty that has totally overwhelmed you and/or that you have taken no steps to overcome.

Here's an example of a good response to this question:

"I think the most difficult thing about being an account executive is making sure no account feels neglected. Everyone likes to think they're top priority; I learned that the hard way earlier in my career when I almost lost one of our biggest accounts. In my zeal to pursue a new account, I neglected to call this key account for two weeks. They thought I had forgotten about them

and was taking them for granted. Now I have a tickler system on my laptop which prompts me to contact all accounts on a regular basis. Key accounts get more frequent attention, regardless of whether there are any pressing issues to handle. I've made it a part of my weekly routine."

15

"IN YOUR CURRENT (LAST) POSITION, WHAT FEATURES DO (DID) YOU LIKE THE MOST? THE LEAST?"

Describe three or four features you liked and one you disliked. Then stop. Often the interviewer will not probe farther. If he or she does, find one other dislike.

Consider the job you are applying for. The features you enjoyed about your last job should be an important part of *this* job. The features you didn't like should *not* be a major part of this job; if they are, you probably don't belong here in the first place. Don't mention problems with particular personalities; the interviewer doesn't know these people and it could type you as someone who has a personality problem yourself.

When mentioning the things you dislike, pick relatively minor parts of the job, and also mention what you did to ameliorate their effect. For example:

> *"It's hard to believe that in a professional position like this one I had to do so much photocopying, but we're short-staffed as a result of downsizing. I'd often use my time at the photocopier to review the latest memo or skim a brief article on my field."*

Never make your last position sound terrible. The interviewer will wonder if any job could possibly be that bad, or whether it's just you who has a negative attitude. She may question why you remained so long in such a situation. She may also wonder if you will talk in similar terms about your new job once the "courtship" is over and you sign on the dotted line.

16

"WHAT WERE YOUR MOST SIGNIFICANT ACCOMPLISHMENTS IN YOUR LAST POSITION? IN YOUR CAREER?"

These questions may be asked separately or together. It's best to pick just a few truly significant accomplishments to discuss in detail rather than reel off a long laundry list of accomplishments that includes your promotion from waiter to headwaiter at your summer job during college vacation.

You will want to pick the accomplishments you wish to discuss based on your perception of the interviewer's "hot buttons" and the description of the job. If organizational skills seem to be paramount, mention a project in which you had to manage people, processes, and deadlines. If leadership has been frequently mentioned, discuss a difficult decision you made in the face of significant obstacles or opposition.

In discussing these accomplishments, a good approach is *problem-action-results* (PAR). State the problem, the action you took, and the results you achieved for the department and/or the organization. State results in quantifiable terms whenever possible. It's stronger to say that you reduced expenses by 15 percent than it is to say that you "significantly" reduced them. Make sure that you can back up this claim or that colleagues at your present or former job would be likely to corroborate it.

Once you have given detailed presentations of two or three accomplishments, stop. If the interviewer wants more, you can continue without seeming to be too boastful or wordy.

17

"WHAT WAS YOUR GREATEST CHALLENGE?"

Pick a situation that reflects significant accomplishment in the face of difficult odds. If possible, pick a situation that was similar to or required similar skills to those needed in the position for which you're interviewing. Use a problem-action-results framework. Stress the results (quantified if possible) that the company achieved as a result of your actions and how you have continued to use these skills in other situations.

Here's an example of a perfectly acceptable answer:

"My biggest challenge was similar to some of the challenges you've outlined for this position. You've mentioned that I would have to give presentations on short notice and think on my feet. At International Bank, I was told two days in advance that I would have to deliver a presentation on cash management to a group of important customers. The scheduled presenter was called out of town on short notice and had no time to brief me. His assistant was very junior and was only of minimal help. So I called a friend who's an instructor at the Banking Institute. She briefed me on the topic and supplied me with additional materials, including some

recent articles. The presentation was a big success. There were one or two questions I couldn't answer on the spot, but I jotted them down and got back to the customer later with the answers."

18

"GIVE ME AN EXAMPLE OF AN INDIVIDUAL WITH WHOM YOU HAD A SERIOUS CONFLICT AND HOW YOU RESOLVED IT."

Choose a situation that was challenging but that you were *able to resolve successfully*. Show how you were assertive in expressing your viewpoint, but also how you were able to listen to the other person's viewpoint to arrive at a win-win solution in which both parties' needs were reasonably met. Illustrate your ability to stay positive during this process and your ability to continue working with this person on other projects and issues. If your relationship was significantly improved by the resolution of this conflict, say so. This can be particularly impressive if other employees found this person particularly difficult to deal with. For example:

> *"I was promoted over a co-worker to become his supervisor. Some conflict was inevitable, especially since he had more seniority and felt he deserved the promotion more than I did. He began to openly challenge me in staff meetings and was dragging his feet on some key projects. I scheduled a meeting with him. I let him know how I felt, but I made some good headway by listening to his feelings and comments, even though some of them were pretty scathing. I felt*

I'd earned the promotion, so I didn't back down or apologize for being in authority. I let him know that I understood how he felt, but that he couldn't challenge me in meetings and that if his projects didn't get done, it was a lose-lose situation, with him probably losing more than me. We also devised some ways for him to expand his skills and responsibilities in the department. It wasn't a perfect solution, but we were able to work together."

19

"WHAT ARE THE IMPORTANT TRENDS OR CUTTING-EDGE ISSUES IN OUR INDUSTRY?"

If you have done your research thoroughly and analyzed the challenges you have already faced on the job, you will be prepared with two or three broad trends that illustrate how well you have integrated this information. You might consider technological challenges or opportunities, economic conditions, the current competitive situation, or regulatory demands. Try to pick trends that were mentioned frequently in your research on the company or that were featured in its annual report. For example:

> *"Based on my formal research and conversations with people in the industry, I see a major trend toward niche marketing. Some firms will specialize in serving large companies, others will go after the middle market, and still others will aggressively pursue small companies with under fifty employees. And there also seems to be a trend toward a 'case team' approach, where a small team located in one place handles a case from start to finish, rather than handing it off to several other teams, each of which performs a separate function."*

To stimulate discussion, you can conclude your answer with a reversal question of your own:

> *"Do you see similar trends, and are you doing any of those things here?"* Or, *"How does that fit with your own analysis of industry trends?"*

20

"WHAT QUALITIES OR SKILLS MAKE A GOOD SALESPERSON (ENGINEER, PROGRAMMER, SPEECHWRITER, ETC.)?"

Use this question as an opportunity not just to identify these skills and qualities, but also to give examples of how you have applied them in specific situations. For each skill or trait, have an example ready. In the case of areas that need development, emphasize the steps you are taking to improve.

Here are two good responses to the question:

"I think a good speechwriter needs a broad knowledge of business, even in areas that seem tangential to a particular company's product or service line. That's why I regularly attend a series of lunchtime lectures at the university's school of business."

"It's no longer enough for an accountant just to count beans after the fact. A good accountant must be a business advisor to the client, making suggestions for operational and fiscal improvements during the audit, not just at the end. In today's competitive environment, an accountant has to be a salesperson, too. I've helped my

firm land one large audit and several smaller ones. I consider myself a salesperson whenever I'm delivering services to existing clients as well. I explain the procedures we are performing, but I always spell out the benefits that will accrue to the client as a result. It's subtle, but it's a definite benefit-selling approach. I want the client to use us not just this year, but in years to come."

21

"WHAT DO YOU THINK OF YOUR FORMER BOSS?"

This is a particularly tricky question. Extol the virtues of your prior boss and the interviewer may think, "How can we measure up to that?" Bad-mouth your former boss and the interviewer will think, "No boss could really be that bad. This applicant has a negative attitude toward supervision; he'll probably be saying the same things about me in a few months."

If you had a good relationship with your former boss, say so and give examples of how you worked well together and he or she developed you. But don't put the boss on such a pedestal that no one else could ever aspire to such heights. "I don't think I'll ever be so lucky as to have a boss like Marge again," may be your true thinking but it can be intimidating to the interviewer and/or your new boss. In addition, you could very well be wrong, since you don't know the new boss well enough yet to make an informed comparison.

If you had a rocky relationship with your boss, first mention the things that you learned from him or her and the example that he or she set. You can say that he or she was well known for high standards and performance demands, and that many employees, including yourself, found it difficult to meet them, but that you performed successfully under these demands and you are proud of your record. You might also say that you managed your relationship with this boss at least as well and probably better than others who worked for him or her. Again, be prepared to give examples.

If your rocky relationship with that particular boss is an exception, mention other bosses with whom you have worked well. (Be honest in your description and examples, since these may be subject to verification during a reference check.) That way, you won't be seen as someone who has a general problem accepting direction and supervision.

22

"DESCRIBE A SITUATION IN WHICH YOUR WORK WAS CRITICIZED."

Everyone, regardless of level, has had his or her work criticized at some point. To answer that your work has never been criticized will immediately brand you as having a poor memory at best, or being closely related to Pinnochio at worst. On the other hand, now is not the moment to mention the time when typographical errors were found in the annual report you supervised, resulting in reprint costs of several hundred thousand dollars. The interviewer is interested in your normal response to a routine criticism. He or she wants to see how you generally respond and what actions you take to improve.

Think of an event that took place several years ago that was moderately serious but turned out all right in the long run. You've had a chance to think rationally about what happened and change your approach to that particular task. Any strong emotional reaction you may have experienced is long since gone, and no one is breathing down your neck about it.

Describe the event briefly and the criticism that was directed at you. Then describe your efforts to improve or change. The best proof that you *have* changed is a recent situation in which you acted differently and this was noted on your performance appraisal or verbally by your manager, peers, or subordinates. It's generally best to state that you've changed significantly but are still working on the objectionable behavior. "If someone tells me they've completely eliminated a behavior, I get suspicious," notes one interviewer.

23

"TELL ME ABOUT ONE OF YOUR FAILURES AND HOW YOU HANDLED IT."

This is a stronger variation of the previous question. The interviewer wants to know not just how you handle routine criticism, but also incidents of extreme adversity. You will want to pick your most significant, impressive failure in which you were able to turn around or at least ameliorate the outcome.

For instance, you may have researched and ordered a software package which proved to be a poor match with your company's needs. However, the interviewer will be impressed if you say that you assumed full responsibility for the error and worked round the clock with the distributor to negotiate your way out of the contract and install substitute software with a minimum of financial loss and inconvenience to the company.

Don't make the mistake of citing an infinitesimal failure such as momentarily forgetting the name of a visiting company officer. Whatever solution you devised won't seem very impressive. And if your failures are this small, how big can your successes be?

24

"WHAT ARE YOUR STRONG POINTS?"

Present at least three that directly relate to the job for which you're interviewing. Use concrete, work-related examples to illustrate these strengths. If the interviewer indicates that he or she would like to hear more, mention another, supplying more examples.

Here's a good and comprehensive answer to this question:

> *"I'm a good presenter. I've been asked to do more marketing presentations than any other consultant in our office. The head of the office said the last one I gave was the best one he's seen this year. I'm also good at proposal writing. I was the lead writer for the proposal that landed us the Big Tech account, which I also presented. And I'm well known for my perseverance and energy in pursuing these tasks. The Big Tech proposal involved working three straight nights until 10:00 in order to get it done on time. There were several team disagreements which had to be ironed out, as well as some technical glitches, but I kept my own and the team's energy up. I never let us get sidetracked from the goal."*

25

"WHAT ARE YOUR WEAKNESSES?"

Discuss one or two. Try to give weaknesses the interviewer already knows about. For example:

"Well, as I mentioned earlier in discussing the Acme project, I'm a big-picture person who sometimes lacks attention to detail."

You will also want to discuss ways in which you compensate for or are striving to overcome the weakness. You might say:

"I always let my administrative people know about this weakness, and I tell them I won't get mad if they double-check small details I supposedly covered—I want them to. I also now make a checklist before every project, no matter how small."

Some applicants like to take a strength carried too far and discuss it as a weakness:

"I'm a workaholic; I get so into the work I have to be reminded to leave at 8:00 P.M." "I sometimes

get impatient with others when they don't live up to my standards of how quickly or thoroughly the work should be done."

The first statement is a transparently obvious attempt to avoid discussing any real weakness; an interviewer we surveyed laughingly offered it as the worst canned answer she ever received. The second one is phrased better and is more believable, but the applicant had better be ready to discuss it in more detail. However, the strength-carried-too-far approach to discussing weaknesses should not be used in a heavy-handed way and in some cases shouldn't be used at all. A sophisticated interviewer may simply continue asking questions until he or she has uncovered several real weaknesses.

Always stop after one or two weaknesses. This is enough for most interviewers. They will wonder what kind of masochist you are if you continue with a long list of weaknesses without being asked.

26

"WHAT WOULD YOUR BOSS SAY IF I ASKED HIM OR HER ABOUT YOUR STRENGTHS AND WEAKNESSES?"

This is a more direct way of asking the previous two questions. Interviewers reason that applicants will give a more considered answer if they believe that the interviewer may actually ask about their strengths and weaknesses during a reference check or other contact with the prior boss. And indeed you should give it a little more thought. The interviewer is asking for your boss's assessment, not yours. Put yourself in your boss's shoes and answer approximately as you believe he or she would. State the strengths first and back them up with examples your boss might use in discussing your performance. For the weaknesses, pick ones you significantly improved in cooperation with your boss, and limit yourself to one or two.

27

"HOW WELL DO YOU WORK UNDER PRESSURE AND MEET DEADLINES?"

This is a dead giveaway that the job involves pressure and deadlines, so if you don't work well under them, this probably isn't the job for you. But to merely state "I work well under pressure" is to beg the question.

Observe that pressure and deadlines are facts of business life. Take examples from your list of accomplishments to show how you have successfully dealt with pressure and deadlines in the past. Think of the worst, most excruciating project, the one that drove you crazy because the deadline seemed so unrealistic. Now it can be a feather in your cap. If you are the person who has actually set or enforced the deadlines, mention this also and give specific examples.

"Publishing wouldn't be publishing without deadlines. There was one author I had to work with who was notorious for getting work in late. I called him several days before each chapter was due to remind him. Not that he always met the due dates perfectly, but he came closer than he ever had before, which my boss said was quite an accomplishment. I planned ahead by clearing my calendar as much as possible and enlisting our best and fastest copy editor and

proofreader. I worked with them shoulder to shoulder for several days. We finished the galleys at midnight the day before they were supposed to go to the printer. That was the first time anyone beat the deadline working with that particular author."

28

"WHERE DO YOU SEE YOURSELF IN FIVE YEARS?"

This is one of the most frequently asked and dreaded questions. (A variation is, "What are your long-range plans?") What if you say you'd like to be the department manager, who just happens to be the interviewer and isn't planning on vacating that position? To envision yourself in a particular position may seem arrogant or unrealistic if your aim is too high—and unambitious if your aim is too low.

A generation ago, it might have been more realistic to say that you'd expect to be one or two levels up in five years. In today's flatter organizations, that may brand you as unknowledgeable. It's better to start by saying that your immediate goal is to perform excellently in the position at hand, and that you would hope that you would be able to grow as you proved yourself and as opportunities opened up in the organization.

You might then use the reversal technique to ask the interviewer, "What kind of career path would be realistic for someone who performs well in this position?" You could also ask how previous incumbents in the position have progressed.

Another approach is to stress the achievements and contributions anticipated in the next five years:

> *"I see myself helping to grow the business, controlling costs and adding to the bottom line in either a line or staff position, depending on the company's needs."*

29

"IF YOU COULD START YOUR CAREER OVER AGAIN, WHAT WOULD YOU DO DIFFERENTLY?"

This is not the time to share major strategic mistakes with the interviewer. You want to present a picture of someone generally satisfied with his or her choices and progress. Who wants to hire an accountant who would become a model if she could do it all over again? What interviewer would be impressed by a bank branch manager who "would have been CEO if only things had been a little different"? Candidates with strong regrets about their career path or who exhibit unrealistic expectations weaken their case.

It's best to talk about minor aspects of your career in discussing "what ifs," and particularly when it comes to things you did early in your career. You might mention that you would have stayed a little longer in your first position to gain more seasoning, or requested promotion a little sooner. You might say that you wish you had moved to your present company a little sooner, since it has been such a growth experience. You could also mention that it is your past, after all, that has prepared you for this position.

30

"HOW WOULD YOU DEFINE SUCCESS, AND HOW SUCCESSFUL DO YOU FEEL YOU'VE BEEN SO FAR IN YOUR CAREER?"

No employer wants to hire someone who sees himself or herself as a failure. Now is not the time to focus on the loss of your previous job as a sign that you are not successful. If you're still working, don't dwell on all the dissatisfactions you may be experiencing at your present job, which you may also associate with feelings of failure.

You can answer this question more forcefully if, prior to the interview, you have done a *success bombardment* on yourself, recounting and savoring at least two or three successful experiences from each job. You can begin with a brief statement that, while every career has a few ups and downs, you're generally satisfied with your achievements and consider yourself successful. You can add that you plan to continue that record with any company you join.

Then you can give a selected description of the successes you've identified in your success bombardment. Present a positive and confident picture of yourself, bearing in mind that an overstatement of your case will be transparent to the interviewer. If you answer, "I'm probably the most successful person I know, and I have never experienced failure in my entire career," you will probably be perceived as arrogant. You will also invite questions designed to pop the huge balloon you have just inflated.

Whenever possible, use measurable business criteria related to the position to define success. One successful candidate answered that success was "developing a carefully worked out business plan and achieving the goals established in it." Another added that success meant going above and beyond the work goals and job description to gain additional responsibility.

31

"DO YOU THINK YOU ARE OVERQUALIFIED FOR THIS POSITION?"

This is a very common question, particularly these days, when corporate downsizing has put many experienced executives in the job market. Sometimes the question can be taken at face value; other times the hidden agenda may be a concern that you are too old or want too much money. Behind the age concerns are questions regarding the applicant's energy level, need for advancement, underutilization of skills with resulting boredom or disenchantment, and length of time you will stay with the company.

Your answer should address whatever concerns the interviewer has expressed directly or indirectly to you, or concerns that you intuitively discern. Emphasize your interest in establishing a long-term association with the organization and say that if you perform well you would assume that there would be expanded opportunities to apply your skills (this is particularly true in a small, growing company). Mention that a strong company needs a strong staff, and if you perceive that the company is rich in youth and energy but a little lacking in experience, say that you could supply that ingredient.

Note that because you already possess so many skills, the company will get a fast return on its investment, and that a growing, energetic company often needs people whose skills can be used in several areas. One of Drake Beam Morin's candidates says, "I mention my overqualification as a positive, since the employer gets more value for the money."

32

"TELL ME ABOUT YOUR WORK SCHEDULE ON A TYPICAL DAY."

The interviewer wants to find out how challenging your previous position has been and how organized and proactive you have been in handling your duties. Are you a clock watcher? Do you seek out others or do they have to track you down?

Of course, you can best answer this question if your job *is* challenging and you *are* well organized and proactive. You can say how you often like to arrive at the office early before the rush so you can read any memos or listen to any voice mail you might have received. If you are a good time manager, you can say that you prepare a prioritized list of projects for the day, or that you prepare it before leaving the office each evening and review or amend it first thing in the morning.

Most probably your job involves a mix of activities, and you will want to make your interviewer particularly aware of any that relate closely to the position for which you're interviewing. You will also want to show how you're able to group and organize those activities: perhaps you like to do written work and reading in the early morning, to schedule meetings in the later morning or early afternoon, and to set aside an hour in the late afternoon to return phone calls.

A weak answer interviewers frequently hear is, "There's

no such thing as a typical day. It just seems like I'm running from one fire to another, trying to pour water on them before they burn the place down." Many applicants believe this response presents them as a person who has many key responsibilities and who can deal with any situation that arises. More often, it only conveys an impression of disorganization and reactivity.

33

"EXPLAIN HOW YOU INTRODUCED A NEW SYSTEM OR PROCEDURE AT YOUR JOB."

Here the interviewer is looking for your creativity and ability to influence other people. If you have never introduced a system or procedure, say so. However, most of us have made some suggestion at work, even regarding a minor procedure, that was subsequently adopted. Anyone applying for a managerial or executive position should have several examples ready.

Use the problem-action-results framework (see page 65) to describe how you introduced the new system or procedure. In particular, you will want to reveal how you evaluated various options, how you persuaded others that the new approach would work, and how you ironed out glitches during the implementation.

Here's an example:

"I noticed that our accounts payable procedure involved five handoffs. One day one of the employees was absent, but the work seemed to go just as smoothly and accurately. When he returned I asked him about his role in the procedure. He replied that it had always seemed redundant to him, but he didn't want to rock the boat or get himself or anyone else in trouble. I

suggested that the operation he was adding could be incorporated into another employee's routine. Today, we have one less handoff in accounts payable. We reassigned the employee to accounts receivable. He calls customers whose payments are overdue to politely remind them. Several of our toughest accounts took the hint and are paying more quickly."

34

"HOW DO YOU STAY CURRENT WITH WHAT'S GOING ON IN THE MARKETPLACE (NEW TECHNOLOGIES, ETC.)?"

You want to position yourself as a professional who is constantly looking for new and better ways to do business and apply technology. Stress the business and technical journals you read (you might cite an appropriate recent article of particular interest), the conferences and trade shows you attend, the professional associations to which you belong (if you are an officer, this is even more impressive). If you have a network of colleagues with whom you frequently exchange ideas, mention this as well.

Here's an example:

"I subscribe to several computer magazines which emphasize business applications. I carry them around in my briefcase, and pull them out whenever I'm stuck on line at a bank or on the train. I also go to at least one national software conference a year, and I'm a member of an informal user's network. The network has people from all kinds of companies, and I enjoy hearing how they're applying the latest technology in their environments. Just when I think we're really state of the art, I'll pick up an idea I never even thought of at one of the meetings."

35

"DESCRIBE A TIME WHEN YOU HAD TO MAKE A DIFFICULT DECISION. WHAT WERE THE RESULTS OF THE DECISION?"

Pick a decision that was indeed difficult and challenging; otherwise the interviewer will underestimate your ability in this area. Also, pick one that turned out reasonably well (the best is one that turned out spectacularly, although the temptation to exaggerate should be avoided). Describe your thought processes, the people you consulted, and how you integrated their advice. Explain how you thought out the impact on particular individuals as well as on the company as a whole. Stress how you worked to magnify the positive results of the decision and reduce any negative consequences or reactions.

Here's an effective answer:

"I had to make a decision to fire someone. It was particularly difficult because this person had made significant contributions to the company in the past, and she had a pleasing personality, which made her very popular in many parts of the firm. However, she was openly disregarding company policies, some of which were essential to our functioning as a team that could meet its numbers. When I confronted her about this, she

denied there was a problem. I met individually with the people who worked with her; in private they opened up and complained that her behavior was holding back the team mission. I also spoke with my supervisor to apprise her of the situation, and to set up a series of steps for the employee to correct her behavior or suffer progressive consequences. I met with her a number of times, but she steadfastly refused to alter her behavior. When I finally let her go, it was no surprise to her or anyone else. The team thought I had handled her fairly, and we were able to move on to achieve our team goals."

36

"WHAT SALARY ARE YOU LOOKING FOR?"

(Variations include, "What is your current salary?" "What kind of compensation package are you receiving?" and "What do you think this job is worth?")

Hopefully, this question will arise after you've had a chance to prove some value by stating how you can benefit the organization. When selling products such as a car, most salesmen begin with all the features and benefits before announcing the sticker price. When selling yourself, you want to do the same.

Never be the first one to bring up salary. If the interviewer brings salary up, particularly early in the interview, don't tie yourself to a precise figure. Too low a figure, and you may have sold yourself short; too high, and the interviewer may be scared away before you have had a chance to prove your worth. You might say, "I understand that the range for this job is between $X and $Y. That seems appropriate for the job as I understand it." You could also ask, "Perhaps you could help me answer by giving me a range for the position or similar ones in the company." If you're asked this question during an initial screening interview, you might say that you need to know more about the responsibilities involved before giving a meaningful answer.

Many interviewers will supply more information about

the job or a salary range. For those who won't and who insist on probing about salary, give a wide range that includes the lowest figure you will take and something slightly above the highest figure you would expect. This will often elicit the comment that you are "in the same ball park," and you haven't committed yourself to a particular figure. Of course, if you are *not* in the same ball park despite the wide range you gave, you're probably wrong for the position, although there may be another more appropriate position available.

If the interviewer continues to probe about your current salary, state the amount you are making now and mention that, like most people, you'd like to improve on it. Note, however, that your major interest is in the job itself and the opportunities it offers to expand and grow.

If a search firm is involved, your contact there will be able to help with the salary question, perhaps even running interference for you. If, for instance, this person tells you what the position pays, and you respond that you are earning that amount now and it would take a little more to get you to move, the search person might go back to the employer and propose that you be offered an additional 10 percent.

Try to defer detailed discussion of salary until you are in the final stage of the interviewing process. At that point, you know that the company is genuinely interested in you and is more likely to be flexible in salary negotiations.

37

"TELL ME ABOUT A SITUATION IN WHICH YOU AND YOUR BOSS DISAGREED BUT YOU WERE REQUIRED TO CARRY OUT THE PROJECT THEIR WAY ANYWAY."

Pick an example in which you discussed your differences with your boss forthrightly and honestly. Show how you presented numerous alternatives rather than merely complaining about the task as presented. Explain how, when your boss turned down most of your suggestions, you turned your attention to succeeding at the task: you were flexible enough, in other words, to adapt your work style and methods. For example:

> *"My boss came up with an idea to change our arrangement with our administrative assistants. Previously, each account manager was assigned a particular assistant. I shared Sam with one account executive, while Mary was assigned to two other account executives. Sam had always liked this arrangement, since he had gotten used to my and the other AE's handwriting, scheduling preferences, and work habits. To tell you the truth, I was pleased to have someone who knew all my quirks, and I wasn't looking forward to using whichever assistant happened to be avail-*

able. I let the boss know this several times, but she insisted it would be more efficient in the long run. It wasn't easy, but I took Sam aside and told him I wasn't sure I liked the new arrangement either, but that we should give it a sincere and honest try. And you know, it hasn't worked out too badly. When Sam's not there, I no longer have to worry about getting Mary up to speed on my projects."

38

"GIVE ME SOME EXAMPLES IN WHICH YOU'VE DONE MORE THAN REQUIRED."

Pick examples that show initiative, but that also show that you touched base with peers or superiors so that what you did was in line with organizational priorities. The problem-action-results framework works very well here, with added emphasis on *your* identifying the problem and acting above and beyond your job description or customary duties. If you received an award or other recognition for your actions, be sure to point this out.

Here is a good response to this question:

"As you know, I'm a technical expert. One day, we received a call from a customer who was having major problems with their MIS marketing and sales program. I generally am not involved in the marketing end of things, and sales is not my specialty either, but the senior consultant who might have handled the call was out of the office and the call was forwarded to me. I listened empathetically for several minutes, made a few broad-brush suggestions on how we might help, and then forwarded the information to the senior consultant, who had since returned. Imagine both our surprises when the prospective

client insisted that I accompany the consultant on the marketing call! I let the consultant do most of the talking, but made a few additional suggestions which were later incorporated into our proposal. That first engagement with that client was for $25,000, and the next one was larger. I like to think that my willingness to do more than required had something to do with that."

39

"IN YOUR PRESENT (LAST) POSITION, WHAT PROBLEMS DID YOU IDENTIFY THAT HAD BEEN PREVIOUSLY OVERLOOKED?"

The key here is not to make the rest of the people in your organization—particularly your manager—look negligent or foolish; you might even point out that you yourself overlooked the problem for a long period of time. Be brief, don't brag excessively. Stress the improvements that resulted from your suggestions or leadership in implementing a solution.

For example:

> *"You know, employment law changes so quickly these days that even experienced professionals can have trouble keeping up. One day I was reading a newsletter article entitled, 'What You Don't Know Can Hurt You.' It pointed out that many companies had questions on their unemployment applications which would have been fine three years ago, but today place them in legal jeopardy. One company in our industry had been sued for several million dollars. To my horror, I realized that we had simi-*

lar questions on our application. I quickly brought them to the attention of the VP of Human Resources and the legal department, and the questions were eliminated from the application form."

40

"TELL ME ABOUT A TIME WHEN YOU WERE FACED WITH A DIFFICULT ETHICAL DILEMMA AND HOW YOU DEALT WITH IT."

This question is becoming more frequent with the increasing emphasis on business ethics and social responsibility, and you can be easily taken aback by it if you have not thought about it beforehand. To answer that you have never experienced an ethical dilemma in your career could cause the interviewer to believe that you are either hedging or that you have never handled any decisions or information of real importance. But you also want to avoid accusing a former employer of seriously unethical behavior.

The best way to discuss an ethical dilemma without divulging confidential information about former employers is to talk about an issue that was public knowledge (internally and/or externally) or that was addressed and resolved successfully by the company. If you have no such example, you might want to use an example from early in your career. If the example is not current, you may be able to divulge the company name. If not, you can state that at "one of your employers" a particular incident happened, but that the name of the company must remain confidential. (Of course, this works best if you've had a number of employers.)

Still another approach, particularly if you have worked for a company well known for ethicality and social responsibility, is to say that you had the good fortune to work for a company that tried not to put employees in positions in which their ethical principles would be put in conflict with company goals. You may then want to discuss an incident relating to your membership or leadership in a community organization where ethics became an issue.

41

"WHY HAVEN'T YOU FOUND A NEW JOB EARLIER?"

(Another variation on this is "How long have you been searching?" with the implication that someone who's been unemployed for six months may not be a top-notch candidate.)

Your answer should avoid any hint of rancor or self-pity. You need to stress that finding a job is relatively easy, but finding a job that makes maximum use of all your skills and is the optimum next step in your career deserves time and careful planning.

Remember that you are just as selective about finding the right job as the interviewer is about hiring the right person for the job. If you've already turned down any offers, you could say:

> *"I did consider one offer, but it wasn't the right situation for me. In the end I'm glad I declined it or I never would have had the chance to pursue this opportunity."*

If your employer gave you a generous severance package, say that you were given ample time to find a new position. Note that you have investigated a number of opportunities (if you've turned some down, mention this also) and that this one looks like a good fit.

42

"WHY HAVE YOU HAD ONLY ONE EMPLOYER IN 20 YEARS?"

This question would not have been asked a generation ago. Most people did stay with a company that length of time. But today, this question reflects the interviewer's concern that you may be used to doing things one way only, that you've taken a passive approach to career planning, that you aren't technologically up-to-date, or that you lack the flexibility to move to another company.

One Drake Beam Morin candidate stressed that her experience was unique in that she was able to participate in several new ventures that allowed substantial personal and professional growth. She showed how these experiences built on one another so that she experienced optimum development while staying with one employer. "In hindsight," she says now, "I should have emphasized the different cultures and reporting relationships I experienced at the company to combat the perception of being effective in only one culture."

43

"WHAT EXPERIENCE DO YOU HAVE ENGINEERING A DOWNSIZING OR MANAGING IN A DOWNSIZED ENVIRONMENT?"

This is an increasingly common question, given all the corporate restructurings taking place. If you have no such experience, you may have a colleague who does and will be able to provide you with some insights before the interview. Alternatively, you can read books or articles on the subject.

If your company did downsize, hopefully the decision was made according to the needs of the business while treating all individuals with respect and dignity. On the company's side this would have entailed communicating the downsizings in a humane and timely manner, providing outplacement or career planning workshops, and giving reasonably adequate severance pay. It would also have meant redistributing work fairly and equitably among the remaining employees, involving them in decisions affecting their work group, and keeping all staff members informed of larger decisions made by top management.

To the degree that your company actually did these things, you should discuss and elaborate on them, along with your personal experiences during and after the downsizing. A manager or employee who has been through a downsizing is more likely to handle change of any kind well. Of course, you may also want to reverse this question by asking the interviewer if his or her company has just completed a downsizing, is downsizing now, or plans to downsize in the near future.

44

"HOW LONG WOULD IT TAKE YOU TO MAKE A MEANINGFUL CONTRIBUTION TO OUR ORGANIZATION?"

This is a tricky question. Even interviewers admit it. If you say you would make a meaningful contribution from day one, you may appear arrogant. (It would probably be unwise for any of us to take meaningful action on our first days on the job, before we have gotten to know the people and culture firsthand.) But if you say, "Six months to a year, once I get to know the organization really well," you run the risk of appearing ineffective or overdeliberative.

A better approach is to say that you have generally adjusted quickly to new situations in the past, giving examples: "This is what I've done in the past to make the initiation process go faster . . ." Say that, while you would expect to meet pressing demands and pull your own weight from the first day, it might take several weeks or months to become fully integrated into the team. Emphasize that you plan to hit the ground running, but you realize that different companies have different expectations about how long it should take an individual to get up to speed. Ask your interviewer how quickly major contributions are expected in this company's culture, and ask for examples.

45

"WHEN YOU FEEL YOUR BOSS OR TOP MANAGEMENT IS OFF TRACK, WHAT DO YOU DO OR SAY, IF ANYTHING?"

The interviewer wants to see if you are so unassertive that you say nothing, or if you are a loose cannon. Think of a situation that you handled constructively and successfully. You probably went through channels, brought up the problem to the proper person at the proper level, pointed out the consequences of not addressing the problem, and made positive suggestions for alternative ways of proceeding.

Here's one approach:

"My boss recently suggested that we do a written survey of all field offices to get their ideas on improving client service. I had just gotten off the phone with several field offices who had complained that Corporate seemed to be "survey-happy." One office manager had similar surveys from Information Systems and Accounting sitting on his desk. I reported this to my manager, who decided to delay the written survey until the offices had a chance to answer the surveys they had already received. For immediate action, she

decided on a less formal telephone survey of one office in each region to get some of the data we needed. Of course, she assigned that to me. I guess that's what happens when you speak up and your suggestions are taken seriously."

46

"IF YOU COULD CHOOSE ANY COMPANY, WHERE WOULD YOU GO?"

It's too obvious to say that you'd come to the interviewer's company. It's also unwise to mention the names of specific other companies, particularly competitors. The best approach is to discuss the *type* of company you'd like to work for. Talk about management style, corporate culture, opportunities for professional growth and training, a chance to work with the latest technology, and other key areas that interest you. As you address each one, make reference to specific aspects of the interviewer's company that coincide with your desires.

47

"WHAT OTHER JOBS OR COMPANIES ARE YOU CONSIDERING?"

This usually indicates that the interviewer has some interest in you and wants to know if he or she might lose you to another organization. However, it may also mean that he or she wants to gauge your judgment or the thoroughness of your job search. This may also be an attempt to learn more about competitors, from whom you may have acquired some useful information during your interviews.

It's best, therefore, not to mention the names of specific companies. Say that you have been to other companies and describe the type of job and the industry. This establishes you as a serious candidate who has other options without putting you in the difficult position of having to discuss other companies.

48

"WHAT WOULD BE YOUR REACTION TO TAKING A PSYCHOLOGICAL TEST?"

State that you have no objection to taking a test per se. However, you would like to know the company's reasoning in giving such tests and why it is important to them. Ask which tests are given and how the results are interpreted (by a psychologist? by a computer printout? by a clerk?). In particular, you will want to know if the interpretation and analysis will be by an internal person or external consultant; external consultants are frequently more objective since they have not met you and will not be working with you if you get the job.

You may also want to know if particular psychological profiles or traits are sought for particular positions. How important will the tests be in determining which candidates are selected? If you are rejected primarily due to the results of the test, will you receive feedback on this? If you are chosen for the position, will the tests be used to further your development on the job, and who will have access to them?

49

"IF YOU COULD BE ANY ANIMAL, WHAT WOULD YOU BE?"

(Variations on this include, "If you could be any kind of material, what would you be?" or "If you lived in the year 1400, what would you be?")

All such questions seek to catch you off guard and get a closer glimpse at the real you. Don't see this as an opportunity to relax and engage in a flight of fancy. You want to give an answer that strengthens your candidacy for this job.

When confronted with the animal question, one candidate replied offhandedly that he'd like to be a baby seal. When he recounted this to his outplacement counselor, she practically clubbed him to death. "A baby seal? A cute little creature that can't survive without its mother? This is a position that demands assertiveness, independence, courage! What were you thinking about when you gave that answer?"

It's far better to answer the animal question with an unusual but impressive choice. This rules out "lion" or "tiger"; both are far too unoriginal and transparent. Instead, think first of the skills and qualities you want the interviewer to see in you, and then of the particular animal that seems to embody them—an eagle for its swiftness and vision, for example, or a dolphin for its resourcefulness and adaptability.

If you are asked a question about what kind of material you would be, and the job requires perseverance and toughness, you might want to answer, "Gore-Tex. It's tough but resilient. It's moisture-proof. Nothing gets through it." And if you're interviewing for a financial analysis or controller position and you're asked what you would have been in the year 1400, you probably want to say an official in the king's countinghouse or head of the royal treasury, no matter how much fun it might seem to be the court jester. You will never really get to be a court jester, but you just might get the job in finance if you present the motivational qualities needed for job success.

50

"WHAT WAS THE LAST BOOK YOU READ? MOVIE YOU SAW?"

Think before you answer this one. The interviewer may just be making small talk, but probably not. More likely, he or she is trying to find out keys to your personality and what you're like after work.

One of the worst answers you could give is, "I never read or go to the movies." This establishes you as a person who probably has no cultural interests outside of work, a one-dimensional bore. But another mistake is to give the name of the paperback you just leafed through in the local drugstore. "*30 Days to Thinner Thighs*" may be a truthful answer, but it doesn't do much to position you for the job (unless of course you're interviewing to be an aerobics instructor).

Try to pick a book or movie that you've read or seen *recently* and can discuss intelligently—preferably one that establishes you as a well-rounded person, a better-qualified candidate for the job, or both. For instance, if you are interviewing for a company undergoing rapid change, you might pick *Reengineering the Corporation* and be prepared to discuss a few key points that might apply to this company. Or you might mention that you just finished reading a book on organic gardening, one of your favorite subjects, but before *that* you read *Reengineering the Corporation*.

Of course your personal life is your business, but questions about reading matter give you an opportunity to position yourself as a well-rounded person who seeks to be informed on professional and general topics. Any movie you pick should also enhance your positioning for the job. If you're interviewing for a responsible financial analysis position, don't identify the last movie you saw as a *Three Stooges* retrospective!

Chapter 3
FOLLOWING UP

Whew! You made it through the interview. You answered all the tough questions—perhaps not perfectly in every case, but to the best of your abilities. You are satisfied that, overall, you put your best foot forward and left the impression of a qualified, confident candidate who answers with candor and judgment. You also thought pretty well on your feet and gave that impression to the interviewer.

Perhaps all you want to do now is sit back and relax or go out with some friends. After all, what's done is done. Well, you probably should celebrate a little. But what's done is not really *finished*. There are still things you can do to bolster your case. The interviewer has probably seen several candidates who are approximately equal in ability, motivation, and fit. Those who follow up appropriately give themselves an advantage over the others.

THE 4-R'S THANK-YOU LETTER

Not more than a day after your interview, write a follow-up note to the interviewer. To help our candidates remember the purpose of the note, we call it the 4-R's Thank-You Letter. The four R's stand for:

1. **Remember:** You want the interviewer to remember you in a positive fashion.
2. **Reinforce:** You want to stress the strengths and accomplishments that seemed to arouse the most interest. You may also want to add another accomplishment that you didn't mention during the interview but that is relevant to the challenges you would face in the position.
3. **Recoup:** In the course of the interview, you probably gave at least one response that could have been said better or that did not give a full picture of your abilities. This is the opportunity to recoup by revising or amplifying your answer. Doing so can help you build even more value and strengthen the interviewer's impression of you.
4. **Remind:** In the last paragraph of the letter, you can remind the interviewer of next steps and any mutual promises made (e.g., "As soon as it comes out next week, I will send you a copy of the article from my company newsletter that details my role in setting up the new computer system. I look forward to hearing from you by next Thursday to learn the date of my next interview.").

Here is a sample 4-R's Thank-You letter:

SAMPLE 4-R'S THANK-YOU LETTER

Mr. John Jones
Vice President
ABC Company
123 Maple Drive
Troy, MI 48084

Dear Mr. Jones:

Thank you for the opportunity to meet with you yesterday.

While I was thinking through the details of the position, it occurred to me that my mathematical programming ability should make me more valuable than the average systems analyst. This would enable you to move more quickly in meeting technical subcontracted deadlines. Also, I would hope that my continued efforts at learning mainframe operations would eventually prepare me for a more central role in your organization.

I am keenly interested in your company and would be glad to come back for further discussion. I will call you next Thursday, as you suggested. Again, many thanks.

Sincerely,

To help you debrief and decide on the content of the letter, analyze how the interview went, including the content and the process. Although you may be very observant and objective, it's often useful to discuss the interview with a friend or a professional outplacement consultant. What went well? What didn't? What answers seemed to cause a favorable reaction from the interviewer? What answers were received unfavorably or with skepticism? Did you feel and act comfortable and relaxed? Did you combine this with an assertive description of your strengths and accomplishments? How would you answer differently if you could have another interview with this interviewer? (If there is one answer that really sticks out, you can amend it in your follow-up letter.)

HANDLING TURNDOWNS

Despite your best follow-up efforts, you may not be chosen to continue in the interview process. This can be very hard to take, particularly if the position seemed ideally suited to you or if you need a position badly due to economic need. For whatever reason, the interviewer did not see you as a good enough match for the position in comparison to the other candidates.

In today's economic climate, you shouldn't take this personally or as a sign that you are not a desirable professional with strong skills. Depending on the level of the position, there may have been anywhere from a dozen to hundreds of applicants, particularly if it was advertised. In such a climate, when a company has narrowed the field to, say, five or six candidates, you have already been judged to be the "crème de la crème."

When they have hundreds of applicants, companies do not waste time interviewing weak or unqualified applicants. The fact that you got an interview speaks to your strong qualifications. In fact, it may be your very strengths or over-qualification that denied you the job. The company has judged that you already possess skills and experience above the demands of the position, and feels it would not be able to give you a position which takes advantage of those skills, either now or in the near future.

You are not a failure because one or more other candidates are a better match for this particular position. You certainly have not been rejected as a person. Most probably the company would have liked to hire several of the candidates, but there was only room for one.

After a turndown, debriefing with friends, colleagues, or an outplacement counselor can help you sort out your feelings, get over them, and move on to the next interview. By talking about your comments and answers during this interview, you can also modify your strategy and approach where this seems indicated.

HANDLING OFFERS

Receiving an offer is a boost to anyone's ego. You've gone through a tough interviewing process against daunting competition and, lo and behold, you were judged the best. Numero uno. First choice.

No matter what your level of expertise or sophistication, it's very easy to lose your sense of objectivity. The company is high on you and you are high on the company. Everyone is feeling friendly toward one another. Your possibilities for growth, advancement, and happiness seem endless.

No matter how good the offer is, do not accept it on the spot. You need some time to think it over, to weigh the pros and cons. Depending on the level of the position and the amount of time you have already talked with the organization, you can usually ask for anywhere from a day or two to a week or two—even more if there will be extended negotiations or a relocation.

Compare the opportunity being offered to what you have now—what you'd be gaining, what you'd be losing. Do you feel comfortable with the organization's culture, its way of doing business, its people, its values? Some candidates even prepare a weighted rating sheet in which they prioritize their criteria for a job, give the criteria proportional weights, and compute comparative scores for their current or former jobs, the opportunity at hand, and any other opportunities they are investigating.

NEGOTIATING

You may decide that you definitely will accept the position. Or you may feel that it is desirable but you can only accept it once certain prioritized factors are altered or resolved. In either case, you will want to negotiate. And the employer will usually expect it. You will never be in as strong a position again as you are in the period between a formal offer being made and your acceptance of the position. This negotiation period is the last step in the "courtship"; once you're on board, your negotiating position will be considerably weaker or nonexistent.

Most interviewers sniff something wrong when a candidate fails to negotiate even one aspect of the employment agreement. Nonexempt employees may negotiate amounts of overtime. An exempt employee can often negotiate salary level within a grade, or time off for college courses. And an executive candidate runs the risk of appearing unassertive if he or she does not negotiate the major aspects of the employment agreement, often trading concessions in one area for gains in another.

In negotiation, the employer is trying to get the most value for the least expense. The applicant is trying to receive the best possible compensation for the value he or she will add to the organization. The key is to maintain a nonadversarial relationship. After all, you will be working with these people, and you will not work well with them if the negotiations have left a bitter taste in the mouth. On the other hand, if you've been a flexible yet firm negotiator, you will set the stage for a climate of mutual respect when you finally sign on.

Often the organization can be flexible in some areas but not in others. And you also must define the areas which are most important to you. Which are "must have's"? Which are subjects for compromise? And which areas are you willing to totally give up in exchange for other concessions?

A common mistake is to focus entirely on attaining a particular salary figure. One candidate turned this into a battle. He kept trying to get the employer to offer more than the employer was willing to do. He was still an unknown quantity, and wanted to come into the organization at a higher salary level than was customary for this position. The employer raised the offer twice, and each time the candidate asked for the employer to double the percentage of the increase. Finally, the employer said, "Frankly, we're feeling a little pushed." Wisely, the candidate answered, "Then I'll stop pushing. I think I'm worth the figure I mentioned, but I obviously haven't proven it to you yet. Can we negotiate a salary review at the end of six months instead of a year?" The review was agreed to, and based on his performance, the candidate was given an increase that far exceeded his original request.

Negotiations usually follow an order, beginning with salary and progressing to other issues. However, like the candidate just mentioned, you may find yourself bringing in other issues to use as negotiating points when salary negotiations have reached a sticking point. Or you may find that you and the employer agree easily on salary and progress so quickly to the other parts of the package that you haven't had time to prioritize them or consider what you want.

Before you enter the negotiations, therefore, it's a good idea to review the entire compensation package, including items that may be important to you that the employer may not even have considered. (For instance, one candidate's outdated computer had just about burned up all its megabytes. She asked the employer to buy her a new one. This was rejected, but the employer gave her the use of a laptop whenever she wanted it.)

Make up a comprehensive list of items that may be negotiable. Then prioritize them, marking each one A (extremely important, must have), B (somewhat important, nice to have), or C (unimportant, give up to gain other benefits). This sets the stage for nonadversarial negotiations; you can avoid becoming locked into an unreconcilable position on any one issue.

This is a good time to clarify the position itself, its responsibilities, goals, power and authority, and other key variables. You may even be able to negotiate a broader scope of power and authority or a bigger title, which will definitely assist you when you begin to negotiate salary and other aspects of the compensation package. We encourage you to review the job responsibilities in a manner consistent with the job level: a nonexempt applicant's review will be less extensive and allow for less alteration of responsibilities than an executive's.

Among the areas you will wish to review are:

- Your principal responsibilities, goals, and mission
- Who will report to you (employees, units, territories)
- The scope of your authority (capital spending, salaries, hiring and firing, organizational changes)
- Whether your authority will be sufficient to fulfill your responsibilities
- What the immediate and long-term performance expectations are, whether they are reasonable, and how they will be measured

- Whether the necessary resources are in place to achieve your goals and if not, how this can be rectified

It is very important to clarify as many of these issues as possible before salary negotiations begin. After all, how can you negotiate compensation in good faith when you don't know the exact job responsibilities and parameters? You may even agree to modify the job description before you begin compensation negotiations so that you and the employer have the same frame of reference. Let's look at some of the key areas for negotiation to help guide you through the process.

Salary, Bonus, and Other Cash Compensation

In most negotiations, base salary is the most important item for both parties. Most of us have certain cash needs below which we cannot live comfortably, and an employee whose cash compensation is below life-style needs often feels unmotivated and underappreciated. In addition, many of us use salary as a scorecard to measure how well we are doing, so ego needs make this issue seem even more important.

It's important therefore to know your minimum cash requirements and also to research the company and the job market to gauge what your skills are worth and to find out the salary range for a position of this type. From your prospective employer, get a listing of the salary ranges for various grades and levels, then compare them to similar positions elsewhere. To do this, consult executive recruiters and friends in your own and other industries. You can also read the *National Business Employment Weekly*, which publishes frequent surveys on salaries for various positions and fields, or consult reference material from the Bureau of Labor Statistics, which is available at your public library.

When negotiating, try to keep the negotiations within a range above your cash requirements. Let's say the employer is offering $53,000, but your minimum cash requirement is $55,000. State that, based on your previous package and what other comparable organizations are paying, you are looking for something within the $57,000 to $60,000 range. If the employer wants you badly enough to meet you halfway, you will agree on at least $55,000. If the company cannot go up to $55,000 due to budget restraints or issues of salary parity with others already in the organization, it may move toward that figure. Since you have compromised in this area, you may then investigate other areas of monetary compensation (yearly bonus, sign-on bonus) to see if the company can bring your actual cash compensation to $55,000 or above.

Fringes and Perks

Fringes and perks mean a lot to some people, in terms of status, power, or money. To some, having the company pay for membership in a health or country club means that they are truly valued employees or executives. For others, it means relatively little; they'd rather have the cash, more stock options, or an extra week of vacation.

You need to decide which fringes and perks are important to you, and which you will trade off against monetary compensation or other perks. Of course, you also need to have researched the company to see which perks are customary at your level and which ones will be a new stretch for the organization. There is also a whole subset of executive perks that ties your compensation directly to the company's long-term performance. These include stock options, equity, and profit participation; by making these a significant part of your package, you deliver the message that you have faith in the company's long-term prospects and look forward to contributing to those prospects.

Relocation Costs

This item is often more negotiable than salary because it is not part of the salary parity formula. Another employee may get bent out of shape if your beginning salary is greater than his or hers, but few people compare relocation costs as a sign that one or the other is more valued or in favor. These costs vary according to distance moved and size of house or family; they are not viewed as signs of personal worth.

Relocation can be very expensive, and many employees don't realize this until they begin to investigate the costs in detail. This is particularly true if you are moving from a low-cost to a high-cost area. A company's willingness to help you with a total relocation package depends on its current policies and how badly it wants you for the position. Study all the costs involved, particularly the differential between what your house will bring and the costs of a similar house in the new area. Be prepared to compromise and offer a reasonable solution that meets the needs of all parties.

If the company has no formal relocation program and it doesn't want to break this precedent, you may ask for a hiring bonus to cover the costs of your relocation.

Quality-of-Life Issues

Many professionals and executives now value their personal and family time as much as time spent at work. They want to spend more time with spouses and children or need time off to spend with aging parents. This coincides with a period in which employers, subject to intense competition and profit squeezes, are not always able to give the large cash rewards, such as salary increases, promotions, and bonuses, that were more frequent a decade ago. Quality-of-life issues may therefore be a significant part of your negotiations, depending on their importance to you. Such issues include:

- Tuition reimbursement or sabbaticals for the employee
- Tuition assistance for the employee's children
- Child- or elder-care assistance, or flexible schedules to allow employees to care for children or aging relatives
- Work-at-home provisions, including use of company computer which is networked into the office
- Job-sharing

These and other such benefits are "easier gives" for the employer because they generally do not have a strong impact on the bottom line. For the employee, however, they often make a major difference in job satisfaction and the ability to balance job and family responsibilities.

Keep in mind that, while many of us like to point to our salaries and bonuses as scorecards of job achievement and financial success, 30 to 40 percent of most people's compensation is in the benefits area (just ask any employer). Your willingness to negotiate in this area could result in a financial package that is more advantageous to your life-style and life goals, even if the salary figure is a little lower.

There should be no surprises in negotiation. As the negotiation seems to be drawing to a close, don't bring up an important item that you hadn't even mentioned up until now, such as the fact that your old employer paid for both your country club dues and your wife's health club membership. This will probably be considered a bad-faith measure, and may even kill the whole deal. It will certainly sour it.

ACCEPTING OR REJECTING THE JOB

As the negotiation draws to a close (hopefully without any last-minute surprises from you or the employer), examine how you feel about it. Did you get most of what you wanted? If you didn't, did the employer make a good-faith effort to compromise in some other area, either now or in a specifically defined future? Did you feel that you and the employer compromised in approximately equal amounts, and that both of you will feel comfortable working together under the negotiated conditions?

If you elect to turn down the job, always do so graciously, particularly if the interviewing and/or negotiating process has been lengthy. State that you value the time and effort the organization put into the process, mention that you were impressed with many aspects of the company and the position, and leave the door open for further contact with the company should a more appropriate position arise. (It's also conceivable that you will be doing business with this company as client or vendor, and you don't want to burn any bridges.) A well-written letter to this effect often leaves a lasting impression. A cold, brief statement like, "I've decided to take something else," will also leave a lasting impression—a bad one.

If, after careful analysis, you decide to accept the job, it is usually best to get an offer letter. While this may seem that you do not trust the interviewer or the new boss, it can be positioned as a way to eliminate misunderstandings. Seeing the conditions of employment in writing subjects them to the type of scrutiny by both parties that is not possible with a verbal agreement and a handshake alone. It gives both you and the employer the chance to perform a final review and iron out any misunderstandings. To the boss who is "rubbed the wrong way" by the request for an offer letter, explain that while you trust him and realize his word is as good as his bond, you would like the agreement in writing in case anything ever happened to him or he no longer was your boss.

The letter should state the nature and duties of the position, the start date, the salary and benefits, and any special compensation or other arrangements that have been agreed to. If you are unable to secure such a letter, you can compose an acceptance letter in which you summarize your understanding of the job, salary, and employment conditions, and mail this to the employer. The letter can conclude: "If I have misstated or overlooked any of the conditions of my employment with you, please notify me before I start work."

While the interview process has seldom been easy, it has become more intense in recent years for a number of reasons. There are many more qualified applicants, particularly for professional and executive positions. The days are gone when any candidate with the basic qualifications for a particular position could get the job as long as he or she didn't insult the interviewer or mention that little manslaughter conviction. The psychological contract between employer and employee has also changed; the employee no longer signs on for life, because organizational priorities may change yearly. Organizations must judge whether the applicant will be able to contribute not just today but also as the organizational mission changes. They must gauge the likelihood of the candidate choosing to leave in a highly mobile society and job market. And they are increasingly concerned about their legal and medical liability should the employee engage in unethical business practices, violent or harrassing behavior toward others, or abuse of substances such as alcohol or drugs.

For all these reasons, interviewers will continue to ask the tough questions identified here, along with many others. Despite the arduousness of this approach, it *does* pay off for them. But there's a payoff to you, the applicant, as well. The tough questions sharpen your verbal and negotiating skills. You are forced to improve the quality of your thinking and the way you express that thinking. And you are forced to do an honest, critical review of your qualifications, interests, strengths, and weaknesses so that any job that you do take is more likely to be a better match.

Interviewing is a process, not a game. By identifying and giving you guidelines for answering the tough questions interviewers frequently ask, this book has tried to prepare you for that process by helping you perform a thorough career analysis. In preparing to answer the tough questions, you have analyzed your strengths and weaknesses, work and management style, successes and mistakes. You are now ready to answer the questions honestly and positively. This will exponentially increase the chances that both you and your interviewer will make an informed decision about your appropriateness for the job. Whatever position you accept as a result of this process, there will be fewer surprises and a greater likelihood that you will achieve job and career success.

INDEX

ABOUT THE EDITOR

CHARLES F. ALBRECHT, JR. is Executive Vice President of Drake Beam Morin, Inc., the world's leading transition consulting firm specializing in change, career development, and outplacement services. He has designed and managed the majority of corporate America's Volunteer Separation Programs, including those for IBM, GM, AT&T, Monsanto, Sohio, and Dow. Prior to joining DBM, Chuck spent ten years with Avon Products, Inc. He is the co-author, with James Cabrera, of *The Lifetime Career Manager*.

ABOUT DRAKE BEAM MORIN, INC.

DRAKE BEAM MORIN, INC. is the world's leading career consulting firm. As experts in outplacement and internal career management, DBM consults daily with major corporations, private enterprises, not-for-profit organizations and governments around the world. With a network of nearly two hundred offices and thousands of consulting experts worldwide, DBM presents an almost limitless resource of up-to-the-minute information in the critical management science areas of careers and change.

From this uniquely rich resource base, DBM Publishing brings to the public material that incorporates this experience, lending it a creditability that no other publisher can match. We are, in essence, what we do and we are committed to providing the best in quality books and materials to meet and exceed the needs of our readers.

LOOK FOR THESE OTHER FINE
DBM PUBLISHING TITLES

Real-Life Resumés That Work!
On-Line Resources and Job-Winning Resumés ($12.95)
Expert advice on how to package job skills and experience for immediate results. Features sample resumés for today's hottest career areas, a wide selection of sample cover letters, a complete listing of on-line job search resources, and tips for preparing electronically scannable resumés.

The First Job Hunt Survival Guide ($11.95)
"An excellent guide for any college student or graduate who is entering the job market. Clearly written, well-organized and packed with the type of information every job-seeker needs."
— Kevin Harrington
   Director, Career Services
   Harvard University
   Graduate School of Education

From Stress to Strength
Achieving Wellness at Work and in Life ($11.95)
Here are proven strategies to identify the sources of stress and move beyond them, and to manage time and energy effectively for a more fulfilling, productive, and balanced life. Includes a personal stress assessment system.

Make Your Own Breaks
Become an Entrepreneur & Create Your Own Future ($15.95)
This savvy, step-by-step guide can help turn your entrepreneurial dreams into a profitable reality. With profiles of 40 top entrepreneurs, this book puts a world of money-making ideas and insights at your fingertips.

Stay in Control
How to Cope and Still Get the Job You Really Want ($14.95)
Hunting for a job requires complete focus, organization, and determination — which is precisely what you'll get from the numerous goal-oriented charts, exercises, and worksheets in *Stay in Control*. So, if you want to take charge and take control of your job search, this is one book you can't afford to ignore.

AVAILABLE AT ALL BOOKSTORES!